THE MATHESON MONOGRAPHS

The principal objective of the Matheson Trust is to promote the study of comparative religion from the point of view of the underlying harmony of the great religious and philosophical traditions of the world. This objective is being pursued through such means as audio-visual media, the support and sponsorship of lecture series and conferences, the creation of a website, collaboration with film production companies and publishing companies as well as the Trust's own series of publications.

The Matheson Monographs will cover a wide range of themes within the field of comparative religion: scriptural exegesis in different religious traditions; the modalities of spiritual and contemplative life; in-depth mystical studies of particular religious traditions; broad comparative analyses taking in a series of religious forms; studies of traditional arts, crafts and cosmological sciences; and contemporary scholarly expositions of religious philosophy and metaphysics. The monographs will also comprise translations of both classical and contemporary texts as well as transcriptions of lectures by, and interviews with, spiritual and scholarly authorities from different religious and philosophical traditions.

THE LIVING PALM TREE

צדק כתמר יפרח

The righteous shall flourish like the palm tree.
Psalms, 92:12 — תהלים צב״ יג״

THE LIVING PALM TREE

Parables, Stories
and Teachings
from the Kabbalah

Mario Satz

Translated from Spanish
by Juan Acevedo

THE MATHESON TRUST
For the Study of Comparative Religion

First published as
La palmera transparente
by Editorial EDAF, Madrid 2000

This translation © The Matheson Trust 2010

This first English edition published 2010 by
The Matheson Trust
PO Box 336
56 Gloucester Road
London SW7 4UB, UK

http://themathesontrust.org

ISBN 978 1 908092 00 7

*All rights reserved. No part of this publication
may be reproduced, stored in a retrieval system,
or transmitted in any form or by any means, electronic,
mechanical, photocopying, recording, or otherwise,
without the prior written permission of the Publisher.*

British Library Cataloguing-in-Publication Data.
A catalogue record for this book is
available from the British Library

Cover: Illumination from the Cervera Bible, c.1300
(Biblioteca Nacional de Portugal, IL. 72)
referring to the vision in Zechariah 4

For Leonardo Senkman,
with affection

Contents

Preface to the English Translation xiii
Preface xv
1. The Aerialist, His Balancing Pole and the Blade of Grass . . . 1
2. The Five Secrets of Happiness 3
3. The Rock and the Creature 5
4. Distances 7
5. On Energy 9
6. The Bubble Laugher 12
7. To Look and to See 15
8. The Three Years and the Root 17
9. Changing Fear into a Mirror 19
10. The Reverse of Grace 21
11. The Law and the Kiss 23
12. The Rabbi and the General 25
13. The Stork, the Old man and the Infinite Night 27
14. Something New for the World 29
15. The Best Reading 31
16. In Touch With the Tree of Life 33
17. The Three Kinds of Human Beings 36
18. Ten Fragments of Beauty 38
19. The Infinite Game 41
20. The Firefly Breeder 43
21. The Value of Tithes 45
22. Echoing Yourself 47
23. The Book or the Life 49
24. The Exact Side of Reality 51

25. Learning from the Ignorants 53
26. All the Names of the Earth 55
27. The Deaf-Mute Singer 57
28. The Intermittent Goodbye 60
29. The Folds of the Heart 62
30. In the Cemetery 64
31. The Two Kinds of Master 66
32. The Sheet of Silence 68
33. The Creator and His Creatures 70
34. The Eager Student 72
35. Enlightenment and Return 74
36. The Tear Phial 76
37. The Mandrake, the Saint and the Retarded Son 78
38. Noah's Fate 81
39. Beneath Every Human Being 83
40. The Desert and the Verb 85
41. The Cartographer and the Orange Blossom 87
42. The Dot and the Line 89
43. Light from the Air 92
44. Perfect Ear and Imperfect I 94
45. The Carob Tree Water Carrier 96
46. When Facing Doubt, Trust the Work of the Universe 98
47. Divine Presence 100
48. The Onion and the Value of Symbols 102
49. The Ear of Cereal 104
50. His Soul Blossomed 106
51. Blessing of the Moon 108
52. Yoshka the Hunchback, Thief of Twitters 110
53. Death and the Thistle 113
54. The Times of the Cherry Tree 115
55. The Best Way 117
56. On the Reverse of the Word Sleep 119
57. The Son of the Sea of Air 121

58. Panting or Inspiring. 123
59. Eliezer Ben Yehudah Surrounded by Words 125
60. Black Fire, White Fire 128
61. Ecstasy under the Vault of Shade 131
62. Sulphur and Musk 133
63. The Root of the Past and the Cup of the Future 136
64. Light for the Nations 138
65. The Master and the Essence 140
66. The Spiral Music of the Olive Tree 142
67. In Every Scroll of the Law 144
68. The Heart of Solitude 146
69. Blood and Image 148
70. The Baker and the Angels 150
71. The Sweetness of Wisdom 152
72. Breathing In Infinity 154
73. The Lightning of Paradise 156
74. The Power of the Listener 158
75. To See the Light, to Be the Light 161
76. Punishment and the Hands 163
77. The Blessing of the Food. 165
78. The Reader of Clouds 167
79. Putting Heart In 171
80. The Living Palm Tree 173
General Index 175

Preface to the English Translation

The joy I feel upon seeing the English version of this modest work, whose aim is to actualise the ancient and quintessential lore of the Kabbalah, is not alien to my interest in the life and work of William Blake, to whom I am so much indebted, and from whom I have learnt that the Bible is, above all, poetry, in the highest and most sublime sense of the word. Blake was a mystic and a man of light, whose language is still cryptic and complex for many. He tinged the English language with wisdom and paradox, but he also brought it closer, even more than it already is by nature and inclination, to the Holy Scripture. It may not be by chance, then, that this volume is being published in London, home to such a loving scholar of Blake as Kathleen Raine. She rediscovered, along the path of symbols and comparative studies, that poetry is in the origin of them both. May she receive, wherever she is, my gratitude for all the fields of knowledge to which she has contributed and handed on. "Words," says the Zohar or Book of Splendour, "do not fall into the void." There is always, somewhere or other, someone who embodies the best of words, and who will succeed, like the masters and students of *The Living Palm Tree*, in breathing into our hearts a more lucid and richer life.

M. S.
Valldoreix, 2010

Preface

According to the vast ocean of Biblical wisdom, the righteous man or the initiate is under the patronage of the most upright of botanical exemplars we can imagine, for, as described in Psalm 92:12, he "shall flourish like the palm tree", *tsadiq ke-tamar yifraḥ* צדק כתמר יפרח, a passage in which *tamar*, the said tree, can also be read as an acrostic of the Hebrew phrase *teshubah mayim rabim* תשובה מים רבים, whose meaning is "answer or gathering of many waters". Between this archaic metaphor, whose origin lies hidden in the night of the Neolithic, and the palm grove that sways in the oasis—a fertile place if ever there was any—a paradisal *locus* is echoing; the place where, either actually or figuratively, we always long to return; for mankind thirsts not only after water as such, but also marvels, even if such prodigies occur, sparse and rare, in the midst of a desert full of mirages, whether ancient or new.

Difficulties never dishearten the true seekers, and the vocation for a higher and nobler life remains constant. As the Sufis have said: "Wherever there are clear waters, men and birds gather to drink." This may be the reason why the keepers of the secret oasis, those among the righteous and initiates, work alone or in community in the pattern of the straight palm tree to comfort those who have been oppressed and contorted by fate. In Egypt, at the margins of the Nile, *renpet* (𓋇), the palm branch, used to refer to cyclic time, to generations succeeding one another; but it was also the emblem of the god *Heh*, the personification of eternity, image of an endless period renewing itself over and over. Later on, this idea would be adopted by the Greeks, especially in relation to the mythical image of the phoenix, and this is evident from the very name of the "date-bearing" palm (*Phoenix dactylifera*). In Ovid's *Metamorphoseis*, it is recounted that this bird, the phoenix (φοῖνιξ), upon realising that the five hundred years of its life span are about to end, makes its nest among the branches of a palm tree, and bringing therein aromatic plants such as cassia, nard, cinnamon and myrrh, sets them alight and dies consumed among them, only to be reborn on the third day in the shape of a small worm. The location where this takes place is called Heliopolis, City of the Sun.

Conceived among dunes, sands, oases and blue minarets, Sufism would bring that heritage under the semantic wing of the Arabic term *tariqah*, which designates not only a green palm, but also a certain rule of life, a way of conscious existence. Dictionaries give us a number of related words: a) *atraqa*, to keep silent; b) *tatarraqa*, to open the way towards; c) *tarq*, the sound of a musical instrument. Regarding that path followed by the righteous—the same one intimated by the architectural palms as they spread their optical fan at Cordova's Great Mosque—the Sufis say that its track oscillates between two complementary opposites: *shari'ah* and *haqiqah*, the external forms or rituals and the inner illuminations. To enter and belong to a brotherhood, or *tariqah*—just as when entering a mosque or other temple—implies, according to Shaykh 'Abd al-Qadir ad-Darqawi,

> "a coming out from the safe place of ordinary existence into the alien existence of search. It means abandoning the private project as a meaning to life, that is, the family, since Allah, glory be to Him, has warned that it is a trap for you. It means abandoning the public project which is society and its promise of future rewards, for the future reward of the seeker is now in the Unseen and after death. It means abandoning the autobiographical project of fame and fulfilment, for the self has become for the seeker an enemy, and remains so until it is transformed into its luminous reality, which is pure spirit, *rūḥ*."

We find the origin of the word *tariqah* in the Accadian *daraggu*, meaning to follow a path—to find traces, signs, and follow them. In a figurative sense, leaving aside its simplest meaning, the Bible would refer to human life as a *dereḥ* or path, thus enlarging the scope of the very same phonetic combination to a linguistic domain of ever-recurring affinities. Such is the universality of this symbol, and the importance of its uprightness—of the ninety degrees angle represented by the palm trunk—that we even find it in places where the tree itself is patently absent. Indeed, in China the supreme idea of *tao* or straight path is formed by two characters: *ch'o*, representing a stepping foot, and *shou*, a head, both of which together indicate a clear and virtuous advance. Now, where palms are actually to be found they are called *tsung*, and clearly apparent within this word is the ideogram that conveys the meaning of taking a master as a model (of uprightness). Accordingly, he who follows the cosmic law, he who advances lucidly, does so not only with his feet, but also with his head.

Palm Sunday branches prefigure, within Christian tradition, and following the myth of the phoenix, Jesus' resurrection after the Calvary drama. It all points in any case to a triumph over the nothingness of death, dust and ashes. Gubernatis says of the palm tree that it is a solar and victorious tree, propitiator of regeneration and spiritual riches; and the Desert Fathers, in the first centuries of Christianity, would willingly abandon the splendour of Byzantium in order to sit by the oases and palm groves of the Thebaid to hear—from the mouths of those who preceded them—what was then, more than a blind belief, a philosophy of life. Not one of the many varieties of existing palms is not of benefit and use to the domestic economy of the peoples who cultivate and tend them. Similarly, no act or teaching of the righteous and initiates—be they Arab Sufis or Hebrew Kabbalists—is ever lost in the void, since they constitute, for those who understand them, promptings to rectification, or mystic landmarks.

The fruitful date palm, symbolising for Arabs spiritual work and that sought-after sweetness which we long to find and share, requires loving care, crossed fertilisations, delicate moonlit pollinations. As Carlos Mendoza reminds us in his *Leyenda de las plantas*, this tree needs to have its feet in the water and its head in the fire, for the second element being an emblem of *ruaḥ* or *rūḥ*, a sign of the burning activity of the Spirit, and the first an intimation of the *nefesh* or *nafs*, the vegetative soul, it is upon the exchange and synthesis between the two poles that the initiate or the virtuous will depend to reach the goal along his path to righteousness. "You know well," says Rabbi Rehumai in the *Sefer Ha-Bahir* or *Book of Brightness*, a text from 12th century Provençal Kabbalah, "you know well that *tamar*, the palm tree, embodies at times the masculine principle and at times the feminine, for its main branch, the *lulab*, is masculine, as masculine is its fruit from the external point of view, even though in the inside it be feminine." Surprised at such a wonder, the master then asks himself: "Is that possible?" and answers: "Dates are, by their seed, similar to woman, since she is in tune with the power of the moon. But the Holy One has created the palm tree male and female, just as it is said in *Genesis* 1:27: 'Male and female created He them.'" We have here, without a doubt, a model of spiritual androgyny oftentimes displayed by the righteous and initiates who operate between rigour and compassion, imparting as they go equal measures of justice and clemency, abstraction and sensibility.

The palm tree has a long and eventful life within the heart of Jewish culture. Employed as a symbol of therapeutic work by the physicians of the intertestamental period, the Romans would strike it on the coin celebrating their conquest of Jerusalem along with the motto *Judaea capta*. There, bent over the ground, a woman's figure laments the sorrowful fate of her people; a fate that would become, in our tragic century, a living hell of crematoria in which millions of innocent souls would burn, scribes and teachers, Talmudists and exegetes, but also child prodigies and musicians, erudites and mothers, grandmothers and teenagers, thus culminating almost two thousand years of persecution, contempt and vexation, without this ever prompting the people of Israel, even for a moment, to abandon their love of the Bible, or their fidelity to an ancestral land in which, coinciding with the discovery of the Dead Sea Scrolls, the tall palms of resurrection would grow again, in Israel and in the *Ein Gedi* of the Essenes. *Netsaḥ Israel lo' yishaker* נצח ישראל לא ישקר: the eternity of this people, their profound errancy, their dispersion and their genius, the use they give to the Torah as a multiplying abacus of miracles and truths, psychic mirror and floating plank amid the centuries-long shipwreck; all these, says the proverb, shall not be forsaken. When, in the year 70 of our age, Jerusalem was on the verge of collapse under Vespasian's armies, upon seeing that heavy clouds of grim slavery and theological storm lay before the political and social fate of his people, master Rabbi Yohanan ben Zacai left the besieged city in a coffin, pretending to be dead and carried by the hands of his younger disciples; as this was happening, one of the most amazing events ever to take place in the fields of knowledge was about to unfold, something comparable only to the survival of the *Gnostic Gospels* by the hand of Theodore the monk, who hid them in an asphalt-sealed urn eight kilometres away from Pachomius' monastery, at the foot of that same hillock where they would be unearthed fifteen centuries later in Nag Hammadi, Egypt, thus preserving for posterity what has been nowadays called "the other Christianity". This amazing fact is none other than *the survival of knowledge above the scorn of power*. Such was achieved by the Chinese people when they preserved their wonderful *I Ching* amidst the book-burning ordered by Emperor Huang Ti; it was achieved by hundreds of Buddhist monks when they kept their sutras from the invading Muslim armies who destroyed the University of Nalanda; and it was also achieved by the Toltec wise men, the *tlamatini*, when, before the twilight of their culture, the Aztecs came to take their place. And it was thus that wisdom proved stronger than war.

Brought by his carriers before the Roman general who was responsible for Jerusalem's siege, Rabbi Yohanan ben Zacai emerged from the coffin as if by a miracle in front of a bewildered Vespasian, and asked him for permission to found an academy, a small school where the Torah could be studied and taught. Its name, Yavneh Yam, will remain in the annals of Hebrew culture as that meeting-point where the temple rite and the priestly offices, bound to space, yield their turn to research and study, both tasks performed within time. It is Yavneh, near the Mediterranean coast, from where rabbis and scribes would come to take charge of formalising the Biblical anthology, some forty years after the destruction of the Jerusalem Temple; it is in Yavneh where they discussed whether the Song of Songs, such an important text for later Jewish nuptial mysticism, would be included in the canon; it is in Yavneh where they collected, formulated and coined the Pharisaic proverb that goes: "If there is no flour, there is no study; and if there is no study, there is no flour," thus instilling in the Jewish mind the notion that it is necessary to accompany every heavenly endeavour and meditative process with physical work or a craft, so that the soul never trespasses the limits imposed by the needs of the body in which it is incarnated.

This collection of parables, stories and teachings brought to light by *The Living Palm Tree* would like to pay fervent homage to all those people—bakers, blacksmiths and coppersmiths, carpenters, tailors, merchants, butchers, dyers, clockmakers since the invention of clocks, and papermakers when the East yielded its secret to the West. And this is why this book seeks to reconstruct with clear syllables the voices of those who—from Baghdad to Warsaw, from Pumbedita to Florence, from mediaeval Granada to 19th century Paris, from Istanbul to Calcutta and from Fez to Livorno—no longer have a voice.

It is not easy to act as a verbal magnet for those flaming particles of wisdom which failed to fall under the wheels of terror and hatred; and even less to evoke the sounds of ancient conversations by the light of the Torah, while stones or bullets are pouring outside. It is not easy to be such a magnet without a trace of both grief and pride. No one has, however, a monopoly of suffering, and by no means the Jewish people, but it must be acknowledged that they have, thanks to their passion for study and psychic exploration, an exquisite inclination towards inner adventure, a certain "art of reading" which, in more than one way anticipates, from within Kabbalistic speculation and through the mysterious code of Biblical Hebrew, many of the most recent scientific discoveries: holograms, fractal theory, Sheldrake's morphic resonance or the concept of superstrings in physics, which seems to give coherence to the four universal forces, from gravity to strong and weak subatomic forces. Is it by chance that we find in the Hebrew term for string, *ḥebel* חבל, the sap of the heart, *leaḥ leb* לח לב, and that as by alliteration we make it into *baleḥ* בלח, a pulsation, a flicker, we ourselves start to pulsate, to sparkle and shine, realising that we are not alone and that we are still, somehow, microcosms within a purposeful macrocosm? "No matter how many knots it has," so the Sufis say, "the string is one," and "Whoever does not learn," the Talmudist wise men add, pointing to the negentropic character of meditation and study, "becomes subject to death." They refer to a study and a meditation whose informative value lies well above ritual and observance.

There is currently a significant body of evidence allowing us to think that the *Zohar*, the highest summit of Hebrew and 13th century Castillian mysticism, was an invention of Rabbi Moses de Leon. Invention or reconstruction, it is all the same, since on the one hand, we are sure that the master did not work in a void, but surrounded by manuscripts inherited through the centuries, and on the other hand, we are also certain that the *Zohar* is right now nourishing hundreds, perhaps thousands of human beings who study its pages and plunge into its secrets. Rabbi Jesus of Nazareth said that "Nothing has power above the Spirit," for, like the wind, it blows and goes where it wants; it thrives on liberty, return and chance, the freedom of its flight and the dance of its whirls. Just so—between plasma and electron clouds—do the characters and actors of *The Living Palm Tree* exist, giving here and there testimony to their enlightenment or received graces, both themselves surprised and surprising us. Bewildered too, that we may remember them, and that we have the patience to listen to them as they recall their findings, free in the heaven of collective memory, alive beyond meaningful words and silences. "When you quote a master," the rabbis hold, "he turns over with pleasure in his grave."

I am not sure now I ever called them to the dark teak of my desktop, nor could I say if I invited them haphazardly into my nights and my days, for if there really exists what our sages call *gilgul neshamot* and Plato *metempsychosis*, if there is anything similar to reincarnation, they themselves may have chosen to visit my tongue and make my hands move to talk of what they loved: the Torah, its poetry and mysticism, its hidden keys and revealed truths. If this was the case, and *it is they who have put me to writing*, I give them thanks for having taught me to look at my surroundings with different eyes, for referring me to the sands of Yemen, to the rose gardens of Iran and the snows of Russia; for bringing me towards the sources of the great European rivers: the Volga and the Danube; for guiding me into the dense forests where they wandered in their meditations, and for teaching me, through parables, and even from the darkest ghettos of the world, that every corner of the earth can be a centre where beauty appears naked, uplifting your mind and enamouring it with her breathing. I give them thanks for the ears of corn and the versets, the rugs and the dunes, the telescopes and the ancient texts, the fruits and the star names, the mountain paths and the beaches, the study houses and the brass lamps, for the display of their sorrows and the emphasis on their happinesses. Thanks, from heart to heart.

Those interested in the secret world of the Kabbalah can refer to G. Scholem's *Kabbalah* (Meridian, New York, 1974); Ellen Frankel's *The Encyclopedia of Jewish Symbols* (Aronson, New Jersey, 1992); and, what is now a classic by Moshe Idel, *L'experience mystique d'Abraham Aboulafia*. As regards Jewish demography in general, from the 1st to the 20th centuries, see the *Atlas de historia judía* (La Semana, Tel Aviv, 1974) and the eight volumes of *Historia social y religiosa del pueblo judío* by Salo W. Baron (Paidós, Buenos Aires, 1968), without forgetting the extraordinary *The Thirteenth Gate: Travels Among the Lost Tribes of Israel* by Tudor Parfitt (Weidenfeld and Nicolson, London, 1987). The reader shall find in *The Living Palm Tree* echoes of Hasidic thought, but also of the Midrash and the Talmud, as well as similarities with the Sufi tradition and Zen Buddhism. These similarities are neither deliberate nor casual: they follow the archetypal recurrences found in any authentic and living spiritual experience.

M. S.
Valldoreix, December 1999

The Aerialist, His Balancing Pole and the Blade of Grass

A Romanian-born gypsy called Dimitri Orlin, who used to earn his living as a highwire walker between Moldavia and Transylvania, stretching his wire from tree to tree and whistling lullabies sixty feet above the ground, would often take his long balancing birch pole to Rabbi Eli Shoshani of Turda, a cooper by profession, who knew how to balance the weights by cleverly inserting tiny lead pellets near the pole ends. These were happy moments for Dimitri, as he could share with the Jew the sweet sacramental wines and the pickled cucumbers, honey cakes in the winter and cherries in the summer. But they were also happy for Rabbi Eli Shoshani, who would leave whatever he was doing in his dark workshop, with one of his apprentices in charge of the forge, and come out to the courtyard to speak to Dimitri.

The Jew would invariably be nibbling a blade of grass, a stick of liquorice root or a twig from a rosebush, or any other woody plant he had at hand. He would even keep it in his mouth as he spoke, to the disgust of his wife and his many acquaintances. One spring day, the Jew offered the gypsy a twig of fennel, but this one declined:

"Thank you, I would rather have my old pipe."

"You don't know what you are missing," said the Jew. "God has more flavours than names, and He hides a scent in each herb, and a teaching in each scent."

"When I am up there," replied the gypsy pointing to the sky where he performed his acrobatic feats, the void space of his hoverings, "I neither smoke nor think, nor can I do anything but hum lullabies. I know that my mother's airy hands are near to hold me if I fall, and I recall her smiling and loving as she was in an age where I did not even know she was blond."

"Have here," said Rabbi Eli Shoshani, holding out to him a stalk of grass. "You never know when a good flavour will protect you from a bitterness."

Years later, ninety feet high in Ploiesti, Dimitri the gypsy's counterbalance pole slipped from his hands, and he was left to his foot skills on a crosswinds afternoon, before the eyes of a thousand persons, unprotected, frightened, and with half a lullaby stuck at the root of his tongue. Remembering he still carried Shoshani the Jew's blade of grass in his corduroy waistcoat's pocket, he took it out and put it in his mouth. Its taste was like a peaceful morning in a mountain pasture, like a dark certitude, and like bright protection.

Upon reaching the end of the wire safe and sound, Dimitri let out a deep grateful sigh. A few months later, back at the workshop of Rabbi Eli Shoshani of Turda, after telling him what had happened, he heard the old cooper say:

"The secret of our support is a recurring point, an instant out of time—the light which between two breaths unveils its purposes within our lungs."

Some Kabbalists hold that our life is always pending from a thread, a strand or nimah נימה *so subtle that it could only be compared on earth to the finest, flimsiest blade of grass. Whoever is able, like the stalks and the stems, to bend without breaking, whoever sways without thus forsaking the clinging law of the soil, has his or her breath,* hei ה, *fully preserved by fate or good fortune, called in Hebrew* minei מניה. *Moreover, long before the Zoharic period—the 13th century—masters would consider the letter* yod י, *present in* nimah נימה, *or blade of grass, to be the smallest dot of the greatest mystery. In all certainty it is around this dot that we also find the delicious* manah מנה *or heavenly food.*

The Five Secrets of Happiness

Rabbi Yosif Barionai of Belgrade used to say to his disciples:

"Happiness has five secrets in correspondence with the five senses.

"The first one is that, as happens to the fire of light within and from the eye, it is bestowed upon itself in the same measure it is given to others. The second, that it makes the surrounding air more breathable. The third, that when it manifests, no matter how brief its outbreak, it reconciles our feet to the ground they tread. The fourth, that at the peak of its intensity it weeps tears of joy; and the fifth, that when it listens to itself it discovers in its own expression the true lightness of life."

After some time, and meaning to endorse his master on this assertion, Rabbi Isaac of Sarajevo quoted the following passage of *Isaiah* 55:12: "Ye shall go out with happiness, and be led forth with peace," thereby making Rabbi Yosif smile with irony.

"Going out with happiness is harder than you would think," he commented.

"Why would you say that?" Rabbi Isaac inquired.

The study house was then wrapped in the darkest winter cold, and a pitiable electric bulb was shedding light on the shabby Talmud volumes, trying hard to outline its edges with flickering efforts.

"Because it requires being content *a priori*, before there is any cause for the emotion."

"Do you know of any method to achieve that?"

Rabbi Yosif Barionai rose to his feet, drew a small mirror from his pocket, placed it in front of his face, broad and entangled with a beard, and sticking his tongue out at himself he added:

THE LIVING PALM TREE

"Every morning I wonder how is it possible that such an organ, the tongue, contains so many wonders, yet it dwells so lonely in its cave of teeth. But since there is no possible answer to this riddle, I start laughing so heartily that I forget where I come from and where I am going. Believe me, my friend, the Creator tied the tongue with the frenulum one instant before it drew our father Adam down to Hell, and He also planted happiness in his heart, so that overawed as he would be, he could still climb out from his depressions through the ascending steps of his senses wide opened."

It has become a proverbial Hasidic idea that when happiness, simḥah שמחה, *appears, it cleanses the five,* ḥamesh חמש, *senses in which it is actually enveloped. For Rabbi Yosif Barionai, the gematric equivalence between the words tongue,* lashon לשון *(386), and void, solitary,* shomem שומם *(386), is a source of laughter, but for some people who lack the sense of humour it is a source of great anguish.*

The Rock and the Creature

Intent on sharpening the minds of his best disciples, Rabbi Yisrael Yabani of Alexandropol gathered them on the eve of the Feast of the Tabernacles and questioned them:

"What do you think is the meaning of 'The Creator is my rock' in Psalms, 18:3?"

The first one to answer was the impulsive Rabbi Yochanan of Abdera:

"The substance of each passage of the Torah is inseparably linked to the numbers of its versets. Therefore, since 18:3 can be read as *ḥagai*, meaning 'my feast', 'my celebration', I understand that the delight of the Creator is His own permanence, the joyous constancy with which He is always present."

"Not bad," observed Rabbi Yisrael Yabani.

"In my opinion," quoted Chaim Joffe of Salonica, dubbed "the student" by everyone, "the rock of God is the firmness on which we rely, the pivot of all our actions."

"Why not think," began Rabbi Yosef Yabani, himself a cousin of Rabbi Yisrael, "that He is the rock against which we crash, the siege that presses our mind, the unflinching solid interrogation upon which is sharpened the edge of all our questions?"

"That is also true," approved Rabbi Yisrael.

Twice again consecutively did the master listen to his disciples opinions. Then, as he poured with his own hands for them a thick coffee, he continued:

"Initially the Creator is for us sheer remoteness, insuperable distance, hardness, and muteness; but when we take the rock in our hands, when we polish its edges, we discover its veins, and we partially intuit the way in which its crystals belong together;

then it becomes our creature, a child of our own understanding; and at that moment—without losing its firmness—it acquires the elasticity we just bestowed on it ourselves."

The psalm in question literally says: eli tsuri אלי צורי, *"God is my rock," translated in numerous versions as "God is my fortress," since this is also one of the meanings of* tsur צור. *However, availing himself of a curious permutation, the master seems to have transposed the letter* yod *within "my rock", placing it in the first place and thus changing* tsuri צורי *into* yitsur יצור, *which means creature.*

Distances

Gathered at the house of Rabbi Yosef of Grodno, four of his most advanced disciples were awaiting the question posed to them every spring by the master. They belonged to the *haburah*, or brotherhood, called *Pri Rimon, The Pomegranate Fruits*, and none of them was above thirty years old.

"Listen to me well," said the master, frowning, while in his eyes glittered that mischievous spark of someone about to set a subtle trap. "This year's question is as follows: What was, in Paradise, the distance between the Tree of Good and Evil, and the Tree of Life?"

The whispers died out, dispersing through the study hall. Birds were chirping outdoors, and the drops of recent rain were still dripping from the eaves.

One answer occurred to the boldest of them, Rabbi Naphtali:

"Four walking days and one entire night. Thickets grew between them both, and carnivorous flowers would blossom. All was danger and ambush."

"Ten *parasangs*," added Rabbi Ishmael the Tall, exhibiting his wide Zoharic knowledge and his vast Talmudic skills. The parasang is an old Persian unit of distance, and it was very likely no one else in the room had the slightest idea about it. It was mentioned in the Talmud, though, and this is why he brought it up. "Ten, like the ten plagues of Egypt."

"The blink of an eye," Rabbi Moshe ben Chaim of Almaty let drop with a triumphant smile, "since they ate with closed eyes, and only upon opening them did they discover the evil they had done."

THE LIVING PALM TREE

"Even though there is no mention about this distance in the Book of *Genesis*," said Rabbi Ezekiel of Riga, "I imagine it must not have been long, since Rabbi Nachman ibn Nejmad of Damascus, in his opuscule *Shbilei Pardes*, *The Paths of Pardes*, said that there is room for the entire Paradise in the heart of the believer. Perhaps one heartbeat comes from the Tree of Good and Evil and the next one from the Tree of Life. After all, they have not ceased beating in our chests since the days of Adam."

Unlike previous occasions, the master did not wait to hear any other answers. He rose, and stretching the forefinger of his left hand, he placed it horizontally between his nostrils and his upper lip.

"The distance between the Tree of Good and Evil, and the Tree of Life is the distance between the nose and the mouth. Some travel it every day, but they ignore its beauties and mysteries, until the moment before their deaths; some others think they know it as they know their faces in the mirrors, but as they recall it they mistake it, and mistaking it they think there is no distance between the trees. Finally, the few know that the Tree of Good and Evil feeds upon the roots of the Tree of Life, but they are unable to calculate the space between both, because in the sweetest moment of their ecstasy they close their eyes to worldly distinctions. To these last, one can apply the teaching of Rabbi Mordecahi of Minsk, who upon his enlightenment sang:

> The musical tear asked to be heard
> by the hand playing the eyelid,
> but the caressing stroke forgot its name."

It is known among many Kabbalists that the distance actually existing between the nose, aph אף, *and the mouth,* peh פה—*given that both words share the letter* pe—*lies in the one spread between the* hei ה *for the mouth and the* alef א *for the nose. It is hence commonly quoted that "the nose is divine and the mouth is human." The Tree of Life does often grow beneath the wings of the air we breathe; the Tree of Good and Evil issues from the foods we eat every day.*

On Energy

On a Warsaw summer's night, two classmates of the study house called *Or Ganuz*, Hidden Light, were discussing Ezekiel 1:4, a verset where the Hebrew word *ha-ḥashmal* החשמל names the substance animating the Chariot, a concept translated in some Bible versions as radiance, in others as energy.

"I suspect," said the youngest, Rabbi Eliezer, "that for the prophet this vision must have been like glancing at an erupting volcano: had he leant excessively towards it, he would not have lived to tell about it."

Looming and water-laden, a storm was brewing over the city, and a light yet pungent ozone smell spoke of imminent atmospheric feuds.

"What if," asked himself aloud Rabbi Mordechai as he nibbled a black cherry, "it referred after all to a joyous epiphany instead of an ominous spectre of disaster? When you turn the letters around, *ha-ḥashmal* החשמל is transformed into *le-simḥah* לשמחה, for happiness."

A flash of lightning ratified his words.

"In that case," Rabbi Eliezer smiled in bewilderment, "the main danger incurred by all those who 'descend in the Chariot' would lie in the difficulty of turning tragedy into comedy, and in knowing essentially which of these two expressive possibilities has more substance, as no prophet or master ever works for himself."

"Look at the light bulb," Rabbi Mordechai began, as he left aside the cherry pit, relishing the aftertaste of the bitter juice and pointing towards the ceiling. It was clear he was following his own line of thought. "It is thanks to its hermetic transparency, to its fruit-like and crystal shape, that light comes down to us. If you placed your fingers directly between the electrodes it would give you some annoyance, and it would not add a whiff of light to your everyday opacity. The light bulb is the vehicle, that lucidity you need to reach in order to be visited, wings flapping, by the lion, the bull, the eagle and the angel."

"There were no light bulbs then, though," replied Rabbi Eliezer with irony.

The broken flashes of a new lightning criss-crossed the window by which the fellow students were talking.

"And yet the electricity or mysterious energy source was there from the beginning, like the lightning you just saw."

"Incidentally," said Rabbi Eliezer to his friend Mordechai, "what do you mean by 'being visited by the lion, the bull, the eagle and the angel'? Wouldn't that imply there are no differences between prophet Ezekiel and ourselves?"

"Names precede beings and objects," replied the cherry-eating one, "but if besides, as in this case, it is their fortune to outlive them, we should search them for the hidden message they originally conveyed. Thus, for instance, the lion was carrying a mirror, the bull a song, and the eagle a detachment."

"I don't follow you," sighed Rabbi Eliezer as he opened the window to let the words of the dripping rain enter the room with greater clarity.

"The lion brings a mirror for you to discern in it, more than your own strength, the art of doing nothing under the shade of the trees, for a single precise action is worth more than gushing and aimless agitation. The bull brings a song for you to dance to your own clumsiness, and for you to learn how to be an acrobat over your own abysses. And finally, the eagle teaches you that detachment from the one you have been is the most elementary requirement of flying, because traces in the sky do not abide in the air you traverse, but within the intrepid heart of him who knows himself a traveller; this is why, if you accept the visits of the lion, the bull and the eagle, and of that duplicate of yourself who is the man-angel in the Chariot, there is no way you can be lost. You can never be lost. You will see a comedy in each tragedy, and in each comedy the shudder of a repressed sorrow."

Because of its gematria, or numeric value, ha-ḥashmal החשמל *(383) equals indeed* gaʿashi געשי *(383), volcanic; and even if it were only for the mention of fire and burning coals in the text ascribed to prophet Ezekiel, Rabbi Eliezer's interpretation should be deemed correct. Rabbi Mordechai's observation is however more acute: ha-ḥashmal* החשמל*, electricity or energy, is made, through alliteration, into le-simḥah* לשמחה*, towards or for happiness. As regards the lion or* arieh אריה *in the Tetramorph, there is no doubt it bears a* rei ראי*, or mirror, while the bull,* shor שור*, includes a song,* shar שר*, while the eagle,* nesher נשר*, is itself a sign of detachment—elevation, vision, remoteness.*

The Bubble Laugher

Having shown little talent for studies, Itzi Faibl Strubel was sent by his father, soapmaker Leib Strubel, directly to the fat and perfume pans where they mixed the substances for the large cakes later to be sold across the Strasbourg region. Itzi was a calm and skinny boy whose breath had been shortened and whose chest had been oppressed by an early asthma. He had a rare skill for sculpting, and in his free time he would carve out zebras, horses, birds, monkeys, little trees and geese from the large cakes of soap. But as these soap shapes were not fashionable in those days in shops and fairs, it did not amuse Itzi's father in the least that he should continue to make them, and even though he did not openly oppose it, he turned a blind eye to it, considering his son little more than a dimwit, and only now and then would he chide him for his artistic hobby.

A rubella epidemic came spreading from Bohemia, a disease that crossed valleys and mountains, taking the children of Strasbourg by surprise in their little wooden beds, as they lay with the downcast countenance of those who do not understand, and the glassy eyes of extinction. Mothers would weep, fathers would come together with the few physicians in the region and, poultice here, emetic and ointments there, in the end some died of anaphylaxis, some went into endless delirium, and most dragged on sickly, without anyone knowing what to do or who to turn to. Safe from the illness, since he had already experienced it in his own body, Itzi Faibl heard the news, and he asked his father permission to visit his little cousin Franz Yosef. After the day's work was finished, he packed in his bag a soap giraffe and what was left of his great-grandfather's gold-framed spectacles, with only one of the empty rims left. When he arrived in his uncle's house, his aunt was whimpering. Itzi Faibl stepped into the camphor-smelling room, a crackling noise made him aware he was stepping on rock salt. There, by the light of a very straight candle, shivering in his bed, was desolate Franz Yosef. Unafraid of contagion, the visitor kissed him and then introduced the giraffe's soap head in a glass of water on the night table, stirred the liquid and waited a few seconds.

"What are you doing?" Franz Yosef asked with a broken voice.

"I am preparing bubbles, creating rainbows."

He drew aside the heavy curtains of his uncle's room and asked his consent to open the window ajar. April's afternoon light streamed directly into Franz Yosef's blue eyes. The soap cake sculptor brought the solitary golden rim of his great-grandfather's spectacles near his mouth, and he burst loudly into laughter, thus moving the air and producing big cheerful bubbles that floated above the sick boy's bed. Bubbles born from the giraffe, and so transparent that they appeared to be huge weightless raindrops, came to hover around this Strasbourg house, where a child, as in many others, was suffering without knowing why. As he first saw them floating before his nose, Franz Yosef had a coughing bout, then an outburst of happiness. Both cousins laughed together, looking at each other without words. They laughed and laughed until the sick boy felt well enough to leave his bed, stand up, and start with ferocious joy chasing the bubble irises. The mess was so big that aunt Elke, Franz Yosef's mother, worriedly came by to see what was happening, wondering what silly business the cousins were up to.

But she froze in amazement as she spotted in Franz Yosef's blushing cheeks the incipient hue of recovery.

"How were you able to do this?" she asked, unaware that a big soap bubble was soaring behind her head. "What have you given to your cousin to make him so happy?"

"Soap bubbles with rainbow sparks, Auntie."

"Impossible," Franz Yosef's mother mumbled.

Once the fever had abated, with his high spirits verging on euphoria, the sick boy added:

"If you look well, Mama, you will see how in each of these bubbles is trapped one of my ailments and pains, all the itches and the annoyances; Itzi traps them and I destroy them."

"And since the rainbow cannot die," continued the smiling son of soapmaker Leib Strubel, "and it is once and again reborn from the water I stir, your son is feeling like Noah after the Flood: making a pact with life—coming to life again between giraffe soap bubbles."

When the townspeople got to know what had happened at Elke's house, fathers and mothers requested the presence of Itzi Faibl, who in one single week used up one soap camel, two rabbits and one squirrel he had kept with some bits and pieces in his father's workshop. He turned them into coloured air bubbles, producing with them translucent globes of laughter, spherical beings which would dissolve in mid-air the despondence of those attacked by rubella, leaving them cleaner than a linen handkerchief drying in the sun on a summer's day.

Years later, when the infamous Bohemian epidemic was but a bad dream in people's memory, if anyone insistently asked Itzi Faibl how he had managed to cure so many children, he used to answer:

"I really don't know, but I have the impression that miracles are as contagious, or even more so, than the illnesses and mishaps affecting us. It is often enough for just one to take place in order for everyone to benefit."

Although young Itzi Faibl from Strasbourg may not have known, a single alliteration of the Hebrew word for soap, savon סבון, *turns it into* be-nes בנס, *meaning* by *or* through a miracle, *and an additional letter* vav ו *representing man. Indeed, oftentimes the latter is healed more by the good intentions of those who love him than by the clever purposes of those who study him."*

To Look and to See

Rabbi Noah Moshe of Antwerp, a diamond polisher, and in his spare time, like Spinoza, a polisher of optical crystals, used to say:

"To look and to see are converging verbs which by their subtle difference reveal when something we are observing is or is not understood."

"Could you give us an example?" he was asked one after the other by his disciples, Naphtali of Brussels and Ariel of Bruges.

The master took a small magnifier out of his pocket, rubbed it against his trousers, and said:

"When I was a child, magnifiers would fascinate me even more than my adult job does, the polishing of optical lenses. It is simply because when you see an object, an insect or a flower larger than it really is, when a sudden sharpness reveals the beauty of proximity, the tenderness of intimacy, then as you move from looking into seeing, your sense of delicacy is increased, and your appreciation of complexity grows. To look is an obvious fact; to see is a profound truth. Looking tends by nature to indolently slip into the homogeneous; seeing, instead, being heterogeneous, compromises the eye in the care of your own steps, and in the attention to your own gestures. The yellow lines in the violet's petal, or the number of scales in a butterfly's wing are, under the magnifier, when the intensity of looking becomes seeing, the best guarantee we can have of what variety and detail have to offer us."

"A guarantee?" asked Naphtali of Brussels, ironically.

"Which guarantee?" smiled Ariel of Bruges.

"The guarantee that we will not take advantage of the commonplace or the tired phrase to turn a blind eye to the novelty of the exceptional; the guarantee that—as Hillel the Sage put it—we will not say 'something is known until it has been known through and through,' and we do know that such thoroughness always demands one further look: seeing the one who looks from the relativity of his observation. Believe me: to look is an obvious fact; to see is a profound truth. Looking is an action that will not start without the involvement of the eye; seeing is beyond the eyelid and the eyelashes."

Looking is in Hebrew histakel הסתכל, *and seeing* ra'ah ראה, *both verbs which, although usually given as synonyms, will still let us discern each one's specific trait: in the first one,* histakel הסתכל, *the root* kol כל *indicates both the part and the whole, but in a general way.* Ra'ah ראה, *in contrast, can change into* arah ארה, *to pluck off, to gather, thus showing that seeing implies becoming part of what is seen and bearing fruits with it.*

The Three Years and the Root

"When I was a young man," rose the voice of Rabbi Reuben of Bucharest, "and I knew nothing about nature, I read in the study house that phrase from *Leviticus* 19:23 which says: 'And when ye shall enter the land, and shall have planted all manner of trees for food, then ye shall count the fruit thereof as uncircumcised: three years shall it be as uncircumcised unto you: it shall not be eaten of.' A sentence," went on before his disciples he who was dubbed Big Heart in a Little Body, since he was short and of frail limbs, "a sentence which, in my opinion, displays much wisdom."

The master and his disciples were on board a train bound for Tirana. The landscape they were crossing was under snow, and the mass of dark trees was awaiting better signs from the sky.

"Those three years relate to the root, to the real affirmation of the tree in the ground fostering its development," said Rabbi Reuben of Bucharest.

"But why three and not two, three and not four?" observed Pinchas, the eldest disciple. "I often find all that numerology tiresome and arbitrary."

The master smiled as he looked through the train window, then pensively rolled his afternoon cigarette and replied:

"Every living thing has its pulse, its cycle, its rhythm of expansion and contraction. It thus happens that during those first three years all the tree's energy is polarised downwards, strongly throbbing towards the depths, the same as us, when we start our studies. In this way the root is looking for mineral love, for salts that will caress its beard until such a time when the certainty of absorption is greater than the consciousness of its place. Following a similar process we must wait months, and even years, for the fertility of the depth to become the gift of the surface, for the spontaneous gesture of our best actions to be able to nourish the spiritual hunger of others. To be sure, sometimes more than three years come to pass before we are able to eat our own Torah fruits, instead of gathering the pieces or crumbs of knowledge handed us by others!"

"Are you suggesting," asked Simeon, another of the disciples of him who was dubbed Big Heart in a Little Body, "are you suggesting that the time consumed in that blind underground labour is inescapable? A human being is not a tree, but moves, is never fixed, travels as we do now. Shall we perhaps, in the manner of cherry trees or rowans, stay for three years in the same place in order for something edible to come out from us?"

Letting out a whiff of smoke, Reuben of Bucharest explained:

"I only know that on my thirtieth birthday I went to spend a summer at my uncle Samuel's farm. I had not seen him since my childhood, and it was he who taught me, recalling the Bible quotation, that the 'Ye shall enter the land' of the *Leviticus* passage has a double meaning: first, to observe what is *below the earth*, meaning the working of the root, the humble task usually neglected by most people; and then there is the application of this same idea to the page we study, for the written signs amount to vegetable seeds, since these too are writing in their lumpy furrows the tasty alphabet of pears and apples. We must time and again go from knowing how to eat to eating what we know; many times, so that for us entering the earth shall be like entering the most beautiful and profound paths of the Torah. What fruit and flower synthesise in the drinking cup has already been humbly analysed by the root, which needs three years to impel towards heaven the power it has been granted by the earth."

> *The* Ye shall enter *from Leviticus 19:23 is but an unhappy and bad translation of the Hebrew* tabou תבא, *ye shall come, ye shall arrive, since this expression—which can moreover be read as* be-ot באת, *in the letter, in the sign—echoes and confirms the Zoharic idea regarding the parallelism between farming rhythms and the reading methods propounded by the Kabbalah.*

Changing Fear into a Mirror

Every time Lo-Yadua, the Unknown Rabbi, remembered the sentence in Proverbs 1:7: "The fear of the Creator is the beginning of knowledge," he would recall a walk with his master, the Ancient of Days, over the wall of Jerusalem's Old City, a walk in which the latter, outspoken as always, told him:

"It is useless to read in *yir'at Adonai* יראת יהוה our fear of the Creator; it seems to me instead that it is His fear. Observe carefully: the text speaks of 'fear *of* the Creator' meaning 'the Creator's fear', not necessarily implying fearing the Creator."

The tone in which he spoke was not sarcastic, but it was pungent, indeed even aggressive. There was no worse enemy for him than fear, and no advisor more selfish than dread. For this reason he had since his youth taken pains to examine the concept of *yir'at* יראת, or fear, finding in it, among the letters which compose it, a mirror or *re'i* ראי.

"The world is our mirror, and our seeing is the frame," he used to say, "the *tau* setting false limits to an effectively unlimited reality."

"What are you proposing?" asked Lo-Yadua, nibbling a thin branch of lavender. "There are no mirrors without frames or without sharp edges."

It was September, the month in which swifts prepare for their departure, and when figs burst ripe with the sweet pressure of their flesh.

"Everything we look at is looking at us, for there is no distance between the light of the world and the one shining in our eyes. Just as you expose your naked intimacy before the mirror, re-dressing your face and fearlessly cleaning up your looks, just so should the universe *become the correcting mirror of your actions*. Isn't it true that if you show anger and scorn to the mirror, it will return it? The same is done by the universe, even if you do not notice; the same is done by reality, even if you do not perceive, between beings and things, and immediately, the exact aping of your gestures and thoughts."

"It may be so," replied Lo-Yadua, "but I still do not understand why our seeing is the frame."

"Neither do I!" laughed the old and crafty master. "But perhaps it may be made clearer by the light of this saying from our Sufi brethren: 'The soul is a mirror whose frame is the body. Turn it around and you will see.'"

The Ancient of Days is directly extracting the word re'i ראי, *mirror, from* yir'at יראת, *fear, in order to weave his parable and bring his disciple to a more intimate and personal understanding of the Bible passage mentioned. The letter remaining after the extraction is* tau ת, *alluding to the world, matter; hence, if we can momentarily dispense with the frame,* the entire universe becomes a mirror.

The Reverse of Grace

Orah the Plant, daughter of the Unknown Rabbi, had trouble understanding what her father meant by *the reverse of grace is repose; the obverse of repose is perceiving life.*

"But aren't we perceiving it all the time? Isn't it an obvious fact for us?"

"I am afraid most of the time," came Lo-Yadua's reply, "we wander through the world not knowing whence we come or whither we are going. Because of this we must, now and then, do as the masters of old said: stop praying in order to think of God. In other words, to see ourselves seeing, to make thoughts stop, and let our senses entirely open their corollas, without choosing anything or fixing sight or hearing, breath or touch, on anything."

"The concept of grace, though, has fallen into disuse, hasn't it?" said Ora.

"Only to our disgrace. Nowadays we only have left what is gracious, which is a comic version of it. A relief at times, but a poor remedy for the abundance of evils."

"Perhaps the word is no longer used because it is ineffective," Ora insisted.

"Grace ineffective?" the Unknown one smiled. "How can that be ineffective whereby we have the most radiant certainty of being, the most beautiful song of light throbbing between our shoulder blades?"

"Father, ellipsis is your speciality. None of your utterances is ever straightforward."

"It may be because the eye is curved, and the ear has its own labyrinth."

THE LIVING PALM TREE

The Kabbalah assigns several meanings to the word ḥen חן, *grace. The first one, from which the Unknown One draws his observation on repose, derives from an alliteration: when we reverse the order of its letters,* ḥen חן *can be read* noaḥ, *repose, rest, quiet, an imperative condition for receiving from the world its loftiest gifts of meaning and transcendence. Now, if we follow the Talmudic commentary, and we read* ḥen חן *as the acrostic of* ḥochmah nisteret חוכמה נסתרת, *hidden wisdom, we can understand why the prize of grace comes to whomever knows how, when, and where to make his heart find repose. The Greeks used to call this quiet* ataraxia, *and the Japanese Buddhists find it through* zazen, *the art of learning how to sit still in contemplation.*

The Law and the Kiss

They say Rabbi Jonah of Cyprus used to proudly hold that: "The Law is a dead kiss; and each kiss is in turn a living transgressor, since from the moment it gives itself with eyes closed it does not know what it is doing." Rabbi Me'ir Yuval of Peking commented, to the contrary: "The kiss is a dead statute if it ignores the living Law which gave it existence." Then the daughter of Me'ir Yuval of Peking came up to them and gave a kiss to Jonah of Cyprus.

"Do you see now?" said the advocate of the kiss. "She does not know yet how to read, and even so, without knowing the Law, she has kissed me."

"You are wrong," the legalist replied. "She has kissed you because I, her father, have taught her the Law which proposes love and respect to elders."

According to Tradition, Moses died through, or because of, a divine kiss, be-neshiqah בנשיקה—*probably a heart attack, a passing considered by masters to be the noblest of all possible deaths. During the Italian Renaissance, Bishop Aegidius of Viterbo, at the time under the influence of the Judeo-Spanish exiles, maintained that such a mystic kiss was, at the moment of dying or even before, proof that the Creator was drawing His Spirit with the same swiftness and diligence with which he had bestowed it at the moment of conception. Furthermore, the root* qen קן, *contained within the word for kiss, designates a refuge, a nest. Meanwhile,* shibah שיבה, *also included in the word in question, speaks of a return, a coming back, as well as suggesting old age—old age considered as a return, and thus favoured with the possibility that, in the moment of transit towards the future life, divine pity shall take care of its creature, starting with the lips. We must highlight as well the profound significance of the syllable* yesh שי, *present in* be-neshiqah בנשיקה, *a root that signifies Being, the Existing One, thus justifying the fact that, according to Genesis 2:27, life proceeds from a breath insufflated by the Creator from His mouth into our nostrils.*

The Rabbi and the General

The Roman general Lucius Sextus came to see Rabbi Tzeba the dyer, and told him he wanted to study with him.

"I am very sorry," confessed the Jew while he moved a jar with his hands all rainbow-stained by his trade. "We do not teach."

"You should not react this way," said the general. "After all, we are the rulers of the earth, including this land of yours we occupy now, thus forcing you to pay taxes. Teach me the Torah, and I shall exempt you from it."

"You will pardon me," replied Tzeba, "but we do not teach."

"But I will pay you well, you will receive a great reward. I need to know what this wonderful book of yours, the Torah, says."

"I am sorry," the dyer said, "but we do not teach."

"Please!" broke out the general, seeing that he would get nothing by force. "I am a man who has travelled half the world searching knowledge, and respecting the sages. Come on, old man, teach me the Torah."

"I am truly sorry, we do not teach," once again replied Tzeba the dyer.

"I beg you," Lucius Sextus then implored, falling to his knees. "Knowing is for me a matter of life and death."

And then, finally moved, the old dyer turned to his people's oppressor, and with extraordinary abruptness he snapped:

"On a Sabbath day two Jews climb up on a roof and they jump down the chimney. One comes out white and the other black. Who is going to wash?"

Astonished, as well as excited by the rabbi's unexpected generosity, the general hesitantly answered:

"The one covered in black."

"No," answered the dyer. "The one who came out black looks at the other and thinks: 'I am clean too, why should I go and wash?'"

"That's right," said General Lucius Sextus.

"No," said Tzeba. "It is impossible for two men to jump down a chimney, and one to come out white and the other black."

"Indeed," agreed the Roman.

"No," the dyer said once more. "It is impossible that, being the Sabbath, two Jews will climb up on a roof and jump down the chimney."

The Stork, the Old man and the Infinite Night

Rabbi Elisha of Tiberias had heard people say that if you manage to find the stork who brought you to the world, and you somehow manage to talk to it, you would know from exactly which part of heaven you came, what was your favourite constellation, and which of the four *ḥayot*, the creatures in the Prophet Ezekiel's vision, governs your life. Like every other story heard in childhood, the passing decades ended up diluting and deforming it, to the point that at his eighty-two years Elisha did not know whether he had heard that storks are long-lived and they turn black as they grow old, or whether perchance he had read that story in the *Travels* of Benjamin of Tudela far back in the days of his youth. In his judgment, there was only one way to make this clear: travel to the Judaean desert, where these birds stopped to rest as they returned to Africa on their way from Europe, then, making use of the meditative vehicle called by the masters *dimayon ha-nefesh* דמיון הנפש, imagination of the soul, try to communicate with one of them.

    When, near Anatot, he caught sight of the fuzzy green hills, and the storks over the fields, his heart started racing. They were walking among unexpected lilies and sparse clovers with a ceremonial gait, but none of them was entirely black. They appeared to have emerged from a dream, embodying the very image of watchfulness and discretion. Elisha took out the apple in his pocket, his shabby book of Psalms, and started softly singing the one set apart for the fairest scenes. Anyone seeing him from afar would have thought a piece of the sky was attached upon his head, so blue and white was the silk of his prayer shawl. He took a deep breath, sat down and bit the fruit. A little later, as the sun set, he fell asleep. When he woke up, he found a black stork so near his head that he was frightened.

"What is an old man like you doing so far from home in the middle of the desert?" the bird asked.

"As I am about to depart this world, I am looking for the stork that brought me here."

"You believe in stories then," clattered the stork.

"It seems to me a genuine believer believes everything," smiled the old man. "Was it you perchance, from whose beak I descended to the life of men?"

"That, I shall never tell you," confessed the stork.

"But you are black, and you surely are long-lived too," observed Rabbi Elisha of Tiberias. "You could help me find her. I am curious to know from which part of heaven I did proceed."

"Nothing easier," answered the stork, spreading its wings. "You come from the darkest of nights, and you are going to the darkest of nights, and in between your life has been a colourful party, in which for every three tears of sorrow there were two of joy."

"Is that all?" the old man inquired.

"No," said the stork. "There is something else: I too come from the night and go towards the night; my share of wonders is smaller than yours, but this has not made me come to your house asking for anything. Beauty is neither measured nor captured; fantasy does not thrive on corroboration, nor fables on their expressive accuracy. Wake up and return, spread the wings of your eyelids, and once more give thanks to the Creator for the span of your flight."

When Rabbi Elisha opened his eyes, the first star was shining on a lilac and salmon sky. Over the rolling hills, no stork was entirely black or white.

> *Masters consider the night,* lailah לילה, *to be truly the highest praise, or* halel הלל, *given by the entire cosmos to the Creator, and this is why entering its bosom at the moment of death, and with Psalm 19:1, which shows the glory of His firmament, is a privilege to be requested by those who love the colourful music of the stars.*

Something New for the World

Abu Salim, a well-known Sufi of Almeria, came to visit Rabbi Yehuda Adalin of Granada, because word had reached him that in his teachings he used to say "every human being brings along something new to the world, something totally innovative."

"Our master Ibn Khaldun," said the Almerian Sufi, "praise be to Allah for having nurtured and nourished him, held that cycles repeat themselves, that history is recurring, and that human beings make the same mistake over and over. If this is truly so, what is this novelty you speak about? What can we bring of new to this old and worn-out universe?"

Rabbi Yehuda Adalin owned a herbal shop in the city market, where he bought and sold goose feathers for writing; and he himself had the reputation of being an outstanding calligrapher, or at least so they said at court. It was the year 1085 of the Hijra, and the recent spring moon shone in a sky of diluted agates just before sunset.

"Consider this feather," confided Yehuda Adalin to his visitor, showing him the quill he was working on. "Think of it in the body of the creature it belonged to. It was light and fine as all the others, and as white as to put to shame the clouds. As you know, geese are amongst us, over the land of the Creator, from time immemorial, which makes it likely that this feather has not changed at all since it first emerged, breaking out from an immaculate dream, from the mind of its Maker. Nevertheless, the directions of its flight while still attached to the wing, the colour of the afternoons it traversed, the sharpness of its barbules, and the flexibility of its rachis under the rain made it different to all others. It is true that identical forms come to the world time and again, but their story and movements do differ."

"I don't understand," sighed the Sufi from Almeria.

"Take it," the Jew told him, "throw it into the air. You do it first, and then I shall do it."

Abu Salim threw the white goose feather upwards and watched as it fell spinning round its axis like a whirl of solid light. Seconds after, the Jew threw it in turn and the feather came down in a different way, though still similar.

"The novelty is not in the fall, but in the flight," observed Rabbi Yehuda Adalin. "Even more, the novelty is in the thrust given to its passage through the air. Such are also our lives. As to falling, we all shall fall, but it is in our hands and will to do it with elegance or din, for the good of the earth or for the ill of the firmament. Have it," he added, offering the feather. "It was experiencing the withering of my hands, and now it has just been reborn for you."

"I shall write to you with it from Almeria," said the Sufi with a smile, "to tell you of the sea you have not seen."

"And I shall answer you from Granada," the calligrapher replied, "to remind you of the perfumes you have smelled."

Because of its numeric value, the Kabbalah considers the word feather, notzah נוצה *(151), to be an equivalent of harvest, recollection, asif* אסיף *(151); it holds that to each of our mental flights and movements corresponds a level of heaven, as also an oasis of inner light,* naveh נוה, *already contained potentially in the feather. During the Middle Ages, for making copies of both the Qur'an and the Torah, either a reed or a quill would be used according to what was available at the time of year and supplies through trade and transactions.*

The Best Reading

Rabbi Daniel Ish Tob of Kiev said: "It is better to read the same book thirteen times than reading thirteen different books."

His pupils looked at him in amazement, for they were standing before the house of the famous Maggid of Karlin, whose library was one of the largest and most comprehensive in the region. So much so that erudite scholars from all over Europe and the East would come there to do their research. The Maggid held one open lesson twice a year, and by way of a system akin to that of the Mediaeval *responsa*, some masters and advanced disciples were invited to take part. After opening the doors of the house, a young man dressed in black took Rabbi Daniel Ish Tob and his entourage to the Maggid. They climbed the dark wooden stairs and reached the loft where the library was located. The green velvety curtains were half open, behind which a fabulous panoramic window could be discerned. Books, large and small, seemed to burgeon, float and overlap in a disorderly order. The master—who worked as an accountant for Count Sverdluk—awaited them by his work desk, magnifier in hand.

He was a man of small stature, but a giant in knowledge. His jacket was unbuttoned, for the library was warmed by a cast-iron salamander stove which threw a reddish light upon the sparse furniture, the worn-out leather sofa and the bookshelves. He asked his guests to take a seat, greeted them following the manners of the time, and then abruptly put the question:

"How many books are there in the Torah?"

"Five," one of them answered.

"And in the whole of the Tanakh?"

"Thirty-nine," replied another of the disciples.

THE LIVING PALM TREE

"Well," the Maggid smiled, "if the dew of your resurrection, the light of your awakening, does not exude from those thirty-nine, then you may as well also read these ones surrounding me, and many others, and you will still remain asleep."

"And you, master, have you read all the books in your library?" ventured one of the less shy amongst the visitors.

"Of course," replied the Maggid. "Most of them only once, but the Torah thirteen times thirteen. Of every twenty-four hours I only sleep five. The remaining time, amidst my usual occupations, I ask my heart to read on its own what the blood brings and takes from it."

The visitors were overcome by a silence provoked both by the master's words, and by the dry crack of a log whose burning embers had collapsed within the salamander. The Maggid had read the mind of his main visitor, Rabbi Daniel Ish Tob of Kiev, who was so pale he had to lean on the shoulder of Rabbi Nahum of Altai to keep from falling. Later, on their way home, one of them observed:

"The problem, it seems to me, is not about reading a little or much, but about teaching our soul to read every one of the needs of our body."

"A man like the Maggid," Rabbi Daniel Ish Tob said finally, "can read with his eyes closed. The matter surrounding him has become for him so transparent, and the Torah something so alive, that his mind journeys through the invisible like the sun through the night of remote distances, without going astray or trepidation along the extent of its course."

> *The number thirty-nine equates the value of the word* ṭal טל, *dew, an agent which, according to Isaiah 26:19, awakens those asleep, since it proceeds directly from the Creator. "For thy dew is as the dew of herbs, and the earth shall cast out the dead." Moreover, thirteen is the number corresponding to the name of the One,* eḥad אחד, *and also to the value of love,* ahabah אהבה. *Hence, loving the book of the One, and being loved by Him, means attaining the number twenty-six, the value of the Tetragrammaton or Ineffable Name.*

In Touch With the Tree of Life

On their way to a wedding in a small town neighbouring Odessa, the very slim Rabbi Haim Leib Raze and his disciples came across a band of Cossacks, most of whom were so tall and strong they looked like moustached ogres. Upon seeing the small party, and without a second thought, they blocked the road with their horses and stopped Haim Leib Raze and his people, who were frightened and knew neither what to do, nor if they would emerge alive from this plight.

"Strong Arm Igor challenges the toughest among you to an arm-wrestling match," said the Cossack who appeared to be the leader. "If you win, you can go on your way; but if you lose, you will have to make the rest of your journey naked, wherever you are heading."

Meaning to protect their master, the disciples looked at each other with bewildered faces. Pinchas was strong, but he was too short compared to Strong Arm Igor; Mendel had broad hands, but weak muscles; and Saul, who had good sinews, fine-looking elbows and a courageous character, had had his fingers covered with chilblains precisely that month of the harsh Nordic spring. The Cossacks' horses seemed restless, and they snorted nervously amongst the smoke and broken light of the torches. An improvised tent was soon set up where the wrestling skills would be put to the test. Rabbi Haim Leib asked to touch the Torah scrolls they were carrying as a gift to the community where the wedding was to be celebrated, and he bent over to kiss the holy book. Then, with eyes half closed, he placed his right forefinger on top of one of the wooden trees of life around which the letters slept.

He decided he would be the one to confront Strong Arm Igor, who looked even bigger as he approached the Jews inside the tent. After silence had fallen before a folding table, and Rabbi Haim Leib Raze and Igor had taken seats facing each other, the slim master said:

"Bring in more light; the occasion asks for brighter colours."

The Cossacks were amused by his joke and they laughed heartily. Igor put forth an arm, white and sinewy, but Rabbi Haim Leib offered only the finger with which he had touched the Torah.

"Take it," he told Strong Arm Igor, and once again laughter roared.

The disciples were shivering. The night itself shrank in the cold. The thaw was already starting outside the tent. When, trusting his strength, Igor clenched with all his soul the Rabbi's forefinger, the tent was suddenly filled with colours. Fuchsias, greens, indigos, oranges, reds and yellows were floating above the heads of the Jews and the skin caps of the Cossacks. The fabric itself of the tent became translucent, to the point that they could make out, sharp and high, the stars, which—as those gathered realised soon enough—also seemed to irradiate colours: magenta, violet, heavenly lilac. Then, superstitious and frightened at what they considered to be a wizard's feat, the Cossacks ran to their horses, only to find that the eyes of their beasts had changed their usual black for light green and vermilion, pale ochre and deep blue.

"May Saint Sergius' iconostasis protect us!" cried the chief of the Cossacks. "Let's run away from this madness, far from these Jews!"

When the danger had abated, engulfed by the night and the colours, the disciples effusively hugged and kissed their master.

"How? How did you do such a thing?" Mendel asked him.

Doing up the jacket he was offered, Rabbi Haim Leib Raze observed:

"Rabbi Asher of Alexandria has written: 'If you are near the Tree of Life, soak one of your fingers in its colours, and spread its grace between power and weakness.' Terror is never beautiful, but beauty can, upon occasion, be terrible."

The wooden cylinders holding and supporting the Torah rolls are popularly called 'atsei ḥaim עצי חיים, *trees of life. Moreover, since finger is in Hebrew* etsbaʻ אצבע, *a word containing both the word colour,* tsebaʻ צבע, *and tree,* ʻets עץ, *we can suppose the master had appealed to a word play or* mitshaq milim מצחק מילים, *among the many known to tradition, in order to perform his illusionist's trick.*

The Three Kinds of Human Beings

Rabbi Salomon Levi of Viareggio gathered his most beloved disciples and told them:

"People are not divided into white, Jew, gentile, ancient or modern, but into those who work for wellbeing, those who work for having, and those who devote their time to being."

They were strolling by the Tuscan Sea, since it was Shabbat. The air was crystalline. Rabbi Naphtali of Siena had just been to visit Cardinal Egidius of Viterbo. They had commented upon Recanati's ideas about the *neshiqah* or divine kiss. The eldest of all, Rabbi Haim Orbetello, an author and a composer, inquired:

"If such a division is moral, the classification is unclear; if it is ethical, then still not clear. Could you further explain for us what you mean?"

"Those who work for wellbeing measure the lands, they dig furrows, they open wells, they raise animals they will later force to return to stables. They do not go far, and they love safe frontiers, the limits of their orchards. Those who give themselves to having buy and collect, they measure and weigh objects. When they observe someone, they consider his anatomy and clothing, the space occupied by the person. They are experts in colours and volumes. If they travel, it is for exchange. Their houses are comfortable but cold, as objects themselves. There are at last those who work for being. Everything in them is remoteness, and a longing for remoteness. They are ready to accept that the stars are the countless eyes of a Deity whose limits they ignore, and their highest task is to console those of wellbeing and those of having, who are oppressed by the excess of work or the weight of possession, and they do so by enrobing their breath in sighs of wisdom. They believe neither in frontiers nor in objects; their best abode is a serene breathing, but their true home is the whole universe."

The disciples looked at each other trying to figure out to which of the groups they belonged. Not far from them waves were steadily licking the dark sand. The flight of a seagull attracted the blue eyes of Rabbi Salomon Levi. A moment after he remarked:

"*Do all your deeds for the sake of heaven.*"

It was a Talmudic quotation known to all, but Haim Orbetello had the impression that it was exactly what the white sea bird was doing in its flight.

From the Mediterranean shores of the Yavne-Yam academy, established in the 2nd century AD around the personality of Rabbi Yochanan Ben Zacai, his disciples would watch the fluttering seagulls, shaḥaf שחף, *of dialogue,* saḥ שח, *whose mere presence refined,* shaf שף, *words and polished meanings.*

Ten Fragments of Beauty

Rabbi Eliezer of Salonica sent his disciples to the sea, charging them:

"Bring me one fragment of beauty, some jewel created by the One without hands or any visible craft. Bring to me some natural work which after all shows how supernatural is this world."

The ten disciples went their way towards the shore on that summer's afternoon whose sky was so full of swifts that the very air was shrieking with joy between their wings. There were few people beyond the harbour, other than two or three fishermen who repaired their nets. The surface of the water was still, as if in a trance.

Rabbi Alexis Moshe came back with a piece of a sponge, Rabbi Naphtali Pidion with a branch of red coral. Abraham Herrera Sofer, the blind one, who had gone in the company of his friend Rabbi Aniel of Polygyros, brought with him a seashell, while his guide was carrying a round roe pouch. Rabbi David of Kilkis, the albino, had in turn found a ribbon of transparent posidonia between the sea-washed rocks. Rabbi Yanis Yochanani of Xanthi, who had very good eyesight, found a tiny violet crab, harmless and acrid like its nest of algae. As for Rabbi Mordechai, renowned for his absentmindedness, he chose a bored stone not to have to search too much, while Rabbi Eliahu of Thasos, a fisherman by profession, brought along a sphere of pressed sand. Isaiah of Lemnos, of small build and always with a smile on his face, found a bristled murex which he kept in his pocket ready to show his master. Finally, Uriel of Edessa found the backbone of a small shark; he felt certain that its dry architecture would delight Rabbi Eliezer.

They laid down the ten fragments of beauty requested by the master on the whitewashed terrace of his house, and they anxiously awaited his judgment.

"Explain to me now," said the master, "why is it that you have chosen what you have chosen."

Stepping ahead of everyone, Rabbi Naphtali Pidion held up his piece of coral saying:

"A minute people lives under the water, and among their calcium houses and their coloured branches they let others live. This is how beautiful I would like our destiny to be."

The master remained impassive, waiting for the second explanation:

"The transparency of this seaweed is the best of virtues," advanced Rabbi David of Kilkis, "as there is practically no reverse to it. It lets you see the same as it sees, and its borders are precise and parallel. This is how fair I would like our character to be."

"Whatever is dispersed by the wind," came in Eliahu of Thasos, "when it has the will to reunite, makes the sphere the most perfect of forms. Thus would I like our families to stay together in peace."

"This murex used to dye royal mantles purple," observed Isaiah of Lemnos, "and now, even dead, even empty, it still pricks with its thorns the space of our admiration. May our beauty be so: real and piercing, rugged and exact."

The master was watching them with a mischievous air, as if waiting for each of them to tell their stories, that he could thereby measure their talents and skills, their sensibility and expressive power.

"This bored stone," said dreamy Mordechai, "can serve both as a necklace bead or as a weight. It is thus that I wish the beautiful not to be apart from the beautiful."

At this point, Rabbi Yanis Yochanani of Xanthi brought out his little violet crab and said:

"Backwards or forwards, little or big," he declared, "as this creature's shell, so may always shine amongst us the twilight hue of Genesis."

Then Alexis Moshe stepped forward, and raising his find said:

"May time flow through us, as the ocean through this sponge, and leave in our hearts sparkles of Eternity. Soft is the profound, and supple."

Rabbi Aniel of Polygyros raised his roe pouch, said nothing, and wept silent tears when the blind man he was guiding, Abraham Herrera Sofer, pointed to the opening in his small seashell saying:

"This darkness is an inner world. But I know that the outer one is constantly bathing in the light of the Most High, praised be His tireless beauty."

Uriel of Edessa came forward, and holding out his shark's frame exclaimed:

"Thorn or bone, ruin or shadow of a ruin, dying is to leave a cage; living, to store promises and dreams. Thus, even once we are gone to the next world, a sign of our endurance remains, a symbol of our continuity."

Having heard each and every one of his disciples, the master stepped forward and said:

"Bring now together all the fragments, place them next to each other, and you will see that the beauty they evoke is greater than the sum of its forms. As the *Sefer Yetsirah* puts it: 'God is the place of the world, but the world is not His place.' Searching for beauty and coming across its reflections is only a minute part of the undiscoverable beauty. Just so, what the sea has left for you is that which its waves no longer have use for; but deep within, most dark and even more marvellous, pulsates that which brought these objects forth."

The Infinite Game

At the Paris National Library, in the room reserved for oriental manuscripts, Rabbi Marcel Kahan was pointing out to Rabbi Philippe Schwab the 15th century Persian edition of the *Mantiq ut-Tayr* or *Speech of the Birds*, a donation to the library from its former owner, Baron de Sacy. Wide open under a glass cover, the manuscript was blossoming in minute spring flowers. Its writing was so clear that Marcel Kahan, the linguist, could read the following passage:

"He has gilded the dice of the stars, that every night the sky may play its options. He has gifted the mesh of the body with diverse qualities; He has put dust on the tail of the bird of the soul, and He has made the ocean liquid as a sign of servanthood..."

Rabbi Philippe Schwab let one of his fingernails run against the glass, admiring his friend's accurate translation.

"And yet," he recalled, "Einstein said 'God does not play dice.'"

"He may have meant to say there are no coincidences," remarked Marcel Kahan.

"If you believe in the game, you believe in the freedom of the unknown," Rabbi Philippe continued, "and chance is for you what the Creator keeps for Himself until the instant prior to every revelation. You throw and He chooses."

"You can also believe in the existence of the die," smiled Marcel Kahan, "without necessarily thinking of the good or the ill of the game. Numbers are not in themselves intentional, though their combinations attempt to be. Who cares if it is five in the afternoon of the first day of the week, that you are thirty years old and I am thirty-three? It is all related, as Attar, the author of *Mantiq ut-Tayr*, would put it, to those 'diverse qualities of the mesh of the body', not to the body itself."

"The six faces of the cube," Rabbi Philippe Schwab began reasoning aloud, "like the six days of the week, relate to an atomic, structural order. Look at the face opposing six. What do you find there? One. Maximum and minimum are in the game two faces of the same. The Creator plays with us; we are His playing board, the space where He plays His combinations."

"If this were so, what would be His die?"

"Do you really want to know?"

"Yes."

"The bounces and jumps of our heart. The cubic rose garden of its blood outflow, the revolving miracle of its return from the feet to the crown."

Under the glass, the beautiful Attar manuscript seemed to quiver as water within water. But this effect was due to the sudden and joyous wetness pouring from the eyes of Rabbi Philippe Schwab.

The Hebrew word for cube is qubiyah קוביה, *whose numeric value, 117, is the same as that of one of the names of the Creator,* El Elohim אל אלוהים.

The Firefly Breeder

As a boy, Rabbi Reuben of Yambol was sent to Botev as an assistant to a beekeeper who also owned some large rose gardens. In order to counterbalance his premature intellectual gifts with some hard physical work, his father, Rabbi Samuel, thought the high mountains of central Bulgaria would give him both vital energy and common sense. The beekeeper was called Resnov, and he had another assistant, a Muslim from Sofia called Rasif, who in no time had made friends with the young Rabbi Reuben of Yambol. By day they would look after the beehives, in the evenings the roses, and by night, during the summer, they would spend their time studying the fireflies, which they both found fascinating.

Rasif would catch them and then let them go, so that his fingers would be smeared with luciferin, which he would later rub onto plants, objects and animals with the intention, he said, of conferring on them the *barakah* or divine protection.

"Allah wants that His light is everywhere a link between men," he told Reuben one night. "Just imagine then, what a brilliant builder would be he who could, like the fireflies, build bridges of light to cross the darkness of night."

As the years passed they stopped seeing each other. Rasif the Muslim never returned to Sofia; he married one of the beekeeper's daughters, and eventually became the most renowned firefly breeder in the Botev region. When they were old, both grandfathers, they happened to meet at a horse fair near Gabrovo. Since that time, and until Rasif's death, Rabbi Reuben of Yambol would receive every two months a few perfumed sheets so full of luciferin that they shone in the darkness like the pages

THE LIVING PALM TREE

of an angelic book. When somebody came to ask for his blessing, he would touch his forehead with a finger imbued with the shiny powder as he said:

"When someone sees you tonight and tells you, 'You have a light on your forehead,' remember that the true light of blessing is between your thoughts and your acts, and that you wear it on the outside only to remember that it proceeds from the inside."

One day, one of his nephews asked Rabbi Reuben where had he got such a strange teaching from, and he explained it had come from a childhood friend, Rasif, the firefly breeder, a Muslim from Sofia.

"Even though its rays differ, the light of God is one. Between their Allah and our Elohim," said Rabbi Reuben of Yambol, thousands of fireflies come and go. What is important is to take from them what unites us, not what sets us apart. He who blesses is not waiting for an answer to his function, since the blessing itself is the answer he expects to hear."

Firefly is in Hebrew gaḥlilit גחלילית, *a word in which coexist bliss,* gil גיל, *joy, and the term* gaḥal גחל, *an ember.*

The Value of Tithes

Abu Shaul of Casablanca, a Torah copyist, a renowned *sofer stam*, used to say:

"In the times of our Moses, when he was a prince of Egypt and he walked among the pyramids and would row on the Nile, and exercised himself in the bow and the whip, the harp and the sistrum; when he enjoyed the favour of the Pharaoh and his court, and he learnt medicine, zoology, botany and astronomy, a shaven-headed priest took him to the school of calligraphy, to show him how the animals entered the writing signs, how the geese folded their wings, how the crocodile opened its mouth, the hawk took flight, the cobra became angry. When, in a temple garden, they showed him the ostrich, whose feathers signify the truth, they told him: 'Of all its eggs, there will always be one it breaks in order to attract the flies and thereby feed its chicks.' Likewise, among your ideas and dreams there must be one which feeds the others. This is the tithe of each living being for the continuation of its being, it is the sacrifice of one part of yourself that the others may flourish."

As a commemoration of this surely apocryphal event, not mentioned in the Talmud or the Kabbalah or the Midrash, Abu Shaul of Casablanca, a visionary and calligrapher, used to gather writing feathers. Northern goose, the eagle from al-Andalus, peregrine falcon, and even a swallow's feather, wherewith on certain occasions he wrote the holy name of the Creator, so that it always returned to his life, he said, across the seas of sorrows and the tormented currents of forsaken love. Even though the Maghreb Jewish scribes used to prefer reed quills to the writing feathers, he remained the exception. He lived until his ninety-ninth year, and it is known, since it was recorded, that his last words were:

"The tongue is the feather of the heart. If it is primary, you shall know where to go; if secondary, who to follow."

The ostrich bears in Hebrew the name of ya'en יען, *whose root, with the course of time, would become* 'anah ענה, *to answer, reply, but also to sing, to praise. Among the Egyptians, the fine ostrich* (Struthio camelus) *feather was the sign of Tmeh or Maat, goddess of justice, whose image presided over the psychostasis or weighing of the souls. Its Biblical equivalent, almost a simple alliteration, and supreme virtue of the Creator, would be the word* emet אמת, *truth.*

Echoing Yourself

They say Rabbi Mordechai Leib of Prague, a friend of the Maharal, went often alone to the Bohemian mountains to perfect his ears with the echo of his own voice, which had to cross waterfalls, rivers, forests and cliffs, graze hills and stroke pebbles before coming back to him. He trained himself in this way to prepare for the "Hear, O Israel," since it seemed to him one could never be proficient enough thereat. He thought human beings are distracted by the hundred voices of folly and the thousand of vanity before really listening to themselves.

"'Hear, O Israel' means above all that we must hear our own actions," he used to say, "to perceive everything our voice gathers on its journey through the world's landscapes."

If his voice came back to him wrapped in pine scent, he would know he was at that time climbing the branches of his own mind towards the cloud-covered sun; should he get a humid and warm reverberation, he would know he needed to weep over his faults. But if it happened that the voice came clearly back to him, he would sing a psalm until, enraptured, he knelt down thinking how much larger would be the reflection of silent thought, compared to the ups and downs and the whiffs of the spoken word and its eventual return in the echo.

One day he was surprised in the forest by a storm so intense and wild that only the thunders and the groans of wind-bent timber could be heard. Rabbi Mordechai Leib of Prague took shelter in a cave, and only came back into the daylight after he had smoked three pipesful. When he came out, the twilight blood was spilt everywhere around, releasing the atmospheric pressure of the summer. So many water canticles and such bird bustle were heard that he was overwhelmed, feeling like Noah after the end of the flood.

"Oh Lord, what an echo there is in your glory, and what an ark you have drawn in my breast for me to save the beauty of this moment!"

Saying which, he repeated the famous phrase in Deuteronomy 6:4, where Israel is prompted to hear, and he added:

"I have heard that change tempers Your purposes, and that storm placates Your humours."

The relation between glory, hod הוד*, and echo,* hed הד*, shows that the former leads man, indicated by the letter* vav ו*, to hear himself, until he realises that the duality, the* du וד*, in which he lives is no more than an outcome of the oscillating movement of the Spirit. And this is pictured here by the letter* hei ה*, which, as is known, occurs twice in the Tetragrammaton, the Ineffable Name.*

The Book or the Life

Rabbi Guy Elimelech of Narbonne was a prodigy of memorisation when he was ten years old, a Talmudic genius at fifteen and a reputable exegete at thirty. But it so happened that when he was thirty-two, he was afflicted by a mysterious disease which prostrated him for one long year in his humble bed, in the back of the tannery owned by Rabbi Uri Sasson, who served as his companion and secretary, and at times read aloud for him. They brought him phosphorus crystals from the Baltic, quail eggs from Saxony, wine from Oporto and clay from the Atlas, but none of these remedies would give the master back his pleasure in learning, or the lucidity he had prior to his illness.

One day a traveller came from Tripoli bringing a strange food he claimed to be just like the manna eaten by the children of Israel in the desert. Rabbi Guy Elimelech tried it, and it turned out to be effective. One week later he was able to go out for a stroll around the city outskirts, and the sky of his memory blossomed like a periwinkle. He watched the creatures of air and land, and he smiled. Once recovered, he asked his friends and companions to find him a way to thank the man from Tripoli for his cure, and when these finally managed to find him after a month's long search, the man told them the medicine had been simply a piece of rice paper from China—having arrived in Libya through the hands of Jewish merchants who sailed up and down the Red Sea—upon which was written the following passage from Numbers 11:17: "But now our soul is dried away: there is nothing at all, beside this manna, before our eyes."

Humbled, and yet grateful for the teaching, Rabbi Guy Elimelech of Narbonne realised that his overly ambitious heart had dried up because it longed for rewards. Ambition was shrouding it, and it was corroded by the pride of prizes, obsessed with triumph to the point that reality was for it a book and no longer reality itself. He remembered that the words of the Bible that he had ingested in that thinnest piece of paper continued with a mention of coriander, and from that day onwards, whenever he came across that aromatic herb, he would remember the man in Tripoli, whose real name he never knew.

"Health without creation is nothing," Rabbi Guy Elimelech, now healed, would repeat. "Knowledge without wonderment is nothing. Beauty with neither light nor herb is nothing. Judgment without delight is nothing. But even less is the man who, knowing the perfume of Paradise, forgets that others have noses too."

Delight, 'ednah עדנה, *is one of the traits of the true sage, whose smile must be able to caress all living beings and things. In this very word "delight", we find the roots of* Eden עדן, *Paradise, and, curiously enough, those of* dan דן, *judgment, judging.*

The Exact Side of Reality

Rabbi Nissim Mitrani of Oujda made hourglasses in his spare time and repaired clocks for a living. His tiny work table was a collection of springs, pins, golden needles and worn-out clock faces. He knew the time in every corner of the world, and this made him candidly trust divine justice, for he thought every man has his time and hour.

"Night falls here today, and it falls there tomorrow; there is no going without coming, nor action without reaction," he murmured, as he turned his favourite hourglass upside down. "Even this elusive flowing matter, each one of its thousands of small grains, will eventually know its right position, the sharpest turn of its tiny fate. And what does the sage do when confronted with this fact? How does he spend his most precious moments?"

His colleagues would look at him wryly, probably tired of hearing him always say the same things; but they kept drinking their mint tea, and were ready to listen to him once again.

"The righteous man takes the side summoned by every moment, and seeks the counterweight, for he loves balance. He can be either a ballast or a buoy, as needed, for he knows that reality is an unfinished sketch, whose definitive version we will never know."

"That can be true of the sand," said Rabbi Abimelech Isaac, looking at Nissim Mitrani's hourglass, "which is ever profane, restless, scattered and barren, but it won't hold for its Creator, who is a constant oasis of meaning, holy in what we know, and holy in what we ignore about Him."

The master who collected hourglasses, the knower of world time zones, finding his listeners to be somewhat drowsy, jumped up, unusually for him, and brought before the eyes of everyone a small pile of silica crystals, saying:

"Here is a small parcel of matter sanctified by its use, subject to solar rhythms, sacralised by numbers. In a like manner, the righteous man inserts himself among men to balance their despair with grains of wonder, and however minute his transparent intervention, however minuscule the excitement he derives, he always has time for a smile coming from the balance's fulcrum. He always has time to say: 'This is the instant of awakening.'"

The master keeps in mind that the tsadiq צדיק *or righteous, as "foundation of the world",* yesod 'olam יסוד עולם*, must actually place himself on the exact,* diaq דיק*, side,* tsad צד*, of reality, not always a grateful duty, since it oftentimes implies mediating between irreconcilable extremes, and being afflicted from both sides of the conflict. The relationship mentioned by Rabbi Abimelech between sand and the profane comes from the fact that they are both written the same way,* ḥol חול*.*

Learning from the Ignorants

Shortly before the October Revolution, the immense lands owned by the Tzar of all the Russias were suffering upheaval and terror. Fields, prairies, estuaries and rivers were filled with *straniks* or pilgrims, with demented eyes and tangled beards. In the forest huts appearances of the *baba yaga*, witch-like supernatural beings, assumed the malevolent forms of lascivious old hags. Hunger was gnawing at the birches, and poverty became so obvious that preachers started saying it showed how close the Kingdom of Heaven had come. Nothing and no one was safe then, but even so, Rabbi Lulik of Naryan-Mar, a trader in White Sea herring, would have the singer Isaac of Tura accompany him to every meeting or political speech he attended. He would listen to the fiery preaching of the metropolitans and the beggars, he would be ravished by the sound of the mystical hum of the blind men's balalaikas, or he would hang around outside brothels, looking for an expression of feminine piety; and he would closely follow market chatter, trying to discern what came from the Creator and what didn't, for he held that in times such as these, heaven spoke through countless mouths.

"I don't understand, Master," Isaac of Tura said to him, "I honestly don't understand how it is that you can listen to insults and imprecations, vulgarities and all the silliness spoken in the markets and the harbours without ever blushing, always retaining instead that seraphic smile. Is there no difference, perhaps, between a good and a bad speaker? Can't you tell anger's rant from a good-hearted man's sermon? What is the eloquence you find in the screams of the whores, or in the weeping of the castrati for the greater glory of their adorable Jesus?"

Slowly refilling his pipe, if they were resting, or loosening the reins of his troika if they were on the road, Rabbi Lulik of Naryan-Mar replied:

"Our sages say that after the destruction of Jerusalem's Temple, prophecy was given to the children and the idiots. For this very reason there are, in all speech we hear, golden nuggets in the nasal voices of the fools, sublime sparks, hidden messages, great truths they themselves are unaware of, but such as are discernible for a good ear. My grandfather, Rabbi Schlomo Ari of Naryan-Mar, used to say: 'Be like sparrows and doves, who find their feast among the crumbs left by others. And be like oil in a puddle, opening for the children rainbows of wonder. Whet your tenderness against violence, and deepen your discernment through the madness of others.'"

"I have heard nothing lately but lowly insults and terrible lies," sighed Isaac of Tura. "I suppose I might need to listen to a hundred obtuse lectures in order to get from them one single correct angle."

"Of course," observed the herring trader, "mountains will always be larger than the treasures they contain, there will always be more chaff than wheat, and more feathers than flight. Remember what the Mishnah says: 'He who learns is not subject to death.'"

All the Names of the Earth

The daughter of Lo-Yadua, the Unknown Rabbi, who was taught Hebrew by her father, once told him she did not understand how the earth could have so many different names, being as it was in reality only one.

"What's the use of having earth, soil, continent, planet? I think calling them by one single name would simplify matters."

"Freedom is in the nuances," replied Lo-Yadua.

"For instance," the girl insisted, "planet includes continent, soil and earth, doesn't it?"

"Freedom is in the nuances," her father repeated. "I am sure that, if you look at the words properly, you will find a reason for each name, which sometimes reflects a space, sometimes a time. Spring soil is not like autumn soil."

"Outwardly," she retorted.

"It is true," said Lo-Yadua, "outwardly. But that is where we live. We are neither moles nor rabbits. And even for them it is different in the winter than in the summer."

"The more names we have, the more diluted reality becomes, it seems to me," the master's daughter answered drily.

"The more nuances reality has, the more our spirit is consolidated," replied the Unknown One. "Our body is formed by the same matter that informs earth. When you discover this, the soil becomes firmer for you, and your own depth deeper. At the same time, this lets you realise that the movement, the course and the constant rotation of our planet are tapped as a beat by the infinite, and that each continent is in turn contained by the sky encompassing it. The same colour has different nuances. It may not be conscious of it, but every single one of its tones knows its place within the scale of its complements."

The Hebrew names for the earth are: adamah אדמה, qarqaʿ קרקע *and* arets ארץ. *In the latter, naming both the homeland and the country, coexist in turn two other concepts:* rats רץ, *course, and the* alef א, *sign of the infinite.*

The Deaf-Mute Singer

At first, Rabbi Yotam of Nehardea used to enthral everyone with the tone of his voice, the melody with which he infused his sentences. And his words kept their appeal for as long as his thoughts were in line with everybody else's, but one day, when he decided to enlarge his lexicon, filling it with Babylon angels and botanic subtleties from India, enriching it with recesses, and extending his mental domains, on that very day people found him to be confusing and long-winded; they avoided his company, and they did not heed his ideas about the ultramarine of lapis lazuli being a trace of another heaven. They marginalised him, and they shunned his mere presence. And then, seeing that no one really would listen to him for more than a couple of minutes, Rabbi Yotam of Nehardea, a master and scribe, stopped talking, becoming mute overnight. Those words, verbs, prefixes and adjectives it had taken him so long to bridle, started by and by to leave his mind due to lack of use. He did not, however, lose his speech so quickly. He learnt to talk to himself, and to tell himself all sorts of stories about the unavoidable loneliness of prophets and the accommodating virtue of the Pharisees, about personal time and time shared with others; but the likeness of an argumentation, and the dragging monologues themselves ended up tiring him, to the point that he remained mute forever more.

When others would sit to weep and sing under the willows, remembering Jerusalem, he took a place near the river to listen to the oars chattering in the water. Not that this habit lasted much, for whoever goes mute once and for all, sooner or later realises that he has stopped hearing properly. And this is how he became deaf as well, and he got to use his hands to express himself, in his shopping and small errands, as he had seen those born deaf-mute go about it. His fingers, previously awkward, turned now into doves, hawks, leaves and cat tails. After some time, his knuckles, forefingers and thumbs were so fast, so accurately dazzling, that he himself, Yotam of Nehardea, would find it amazing that these were his own hands. He learnt how to feel the works of his own heart, placing his hands on his chest; and he took the habit, after feeling the heart beating under his palms, to throw his heartbeats into the air as he smiled, returning them to the heavenly course they came from, so that the sun and moon would not entirely waste the treasure of their rhythms. Soon afterwards he deciphered what his eyelids were telling every time he stroked them with his fingertips, and later on he was able to discern, as he blew on his palms, two or three different temperatures in his breath. As soon as he perceived something new, he would return it to heaven with prompt gratitude.

Drawn by this subtle and expressive language, those who had stopped listening to him came back. They were most amazed by the accuracy and the grace displayed as his fingers turned.

At first they were three, then five, and finally the onlookers could be counted by the dozen. Some thought his eloquence sublime, others that he said nothing special, but such was his elegance and perfection that they were reminded of Moses in the initiatic desert of his long journeys. By then, Rabbi Yotam of Nehardea had made for himself a world within the world; he had no need of anyone, and one single steady thought filled his nights and days: "He who was unheard when he spoke is now a master of the silent air. He who makes an art out of the verbal rejection that secluded him, comes to interpret what the silence wants to be known."

Rabbi Yotam of Nehardea died when he was eighty-eight years old, while sitting at his front door in the saddlers' quarter. It happened in the month of Nisan, when the grass is tender, and the lilies announce clearer weathers. Five swallows drew his name on the sky, but no one except him, just an instant before expiring, could decipher the syllabic writing of their flight, and how extreme remoteness had become his most joyous intimacy.

Mario Satz

Kabbalists speak of a certain "returning light", or ḥozer חוזר, *meaning both the matter which radiates the very light that created it, and the highest mission of the student. In the Hebrew verb to return,* lehaḥzir להחזיר, *we find, incidentally, the root* zohar זהר, *splendour, and also* hel הל, *halo, aura.*

The Intermittent Goodbye

"If you pay attention," Rabbi Mordechai of Lisbon commented to his sons, "when we meet others, just as when we part from them, we say in Hebrew *shalom*. Do you know why?"

"Surely to express our desire for peace, our will for the relation established with others to be one governed by serenity, not by tension."

"I believe, father," said the eldest son, "that we say *shalom* שלום so that His Name, *shem* שם, that of the Creator, *lo* לו, is always amongst us."

"The prophet Isaiah compares peace with a river," said Rabbi Mordechai Morteira, pointing to the waters of the Tejo, "and this because it is always fluent and fertile, nutritious and humble, for all rivers bow down before the sea."

"Perhaps we say *shalom*," remarked the younger of the sons, "because life itself is an intermittent goodbye, and we are always somehow parting from someone or something."

"It seems to me," said his next in age, "that it is impossible to know exactly, when we greet others, whether it is the first or the last time we meet."

"Why do you say that?" Rabbi Mordechai was curious to know.

"Because if the prophet is right—and with him also Heraclitus, the Greek philosopher who said 'we never drink twice from the same river'—we are different at each of our meetings to what we were in a previous moment, and thus we choose to welcome and bid farewell with peace to those unknown aspects of known faces that we happen to be shown, so that the unexpected will not disturb the human landscape we were familiar with."

"Peace, then, be upon us and upon everybody," said the rabbi.

"A difficult project facing an all too easy contempt," added his eldest son bitterly, remembering that the Jews had been expelled from Spain, and they would soon be expelled from Portugal as well.

The sentence in Isaiah 48:18: "Then had thy peace been as a river," includes the expression ke-nahar כנהר, *where we find on the one hand the affirmative "yes",* ken כן, *for fluidity, and on the other hand* rakh רך, *something tender, weak, inconsistent. Hence, human dealings need to invoke peace again and again, to compensate for each of the afflictions caused by inevitable conflict and scorn.*

The Folds of the Heart

Distressed and red-eyed like someone who has not slept for days, Zevi Agudo, a tradesman from Milano, made his way to Florence in order to seek the advice of Rabbi Alessandro Luzzato, who used to teach in the study house next to the synagogue.

"Master," he said, "make my journey worth its while; help me calm down my mind."

"What is wrong with you, Zevi?" answered Rabbi Alessandro Luzzato while still browsing through a volume of the Talmud. Easter was imminent, and the first yellow chrysanthemums were blossoming near Fiesole.

"I have felt the claws of loneliness upon me, its dull iron nails, its cork-like shield, its sorrowful emptiness at all times. This is more than enough to make one deranged."

"Why?" inquired the master looking into his eyes.

"That is what I ask myself, since I have family, friends, a job, and I am actually not alone for more than a few minutes a day."

"Are you familiar with the story of Pinchas Deshe, the wandering companion of Honi the Circle-Maker?"

"No, master."

"It so happened that when once he felt lonelier than a summer cloud, lonelier than a deer before the abyss of a starless night, lonelier than a desert spring, lonelier than an abandoned nest or an empty snail shell, lonelier than crumbs of bread scattered under the moon, he went up to his friend Samuel's vineyard, where he fell asleep wrapped in the afternoon drowse. It was there, they say, that he had an illuminating dream. The vine tendrils cradled him, and he became a tiny grape, then another, and then yet another, until he felt like an entire bunch. Immediately, faster than it takes a sigh to leave the nose, he was crushed by the winepress, becoming must, then wine, and finally, when he was about to be drunk, he woke up startled. When he told his friend Samuel about the dream, he wanted to know what was the face of the drinker. Poor Pinchas Deshe, still frightened, replied: 'That is exactly the point: *he had no face.*' Full of excitement, Samuel asked where he had reclined, where he had lain down, then went there and stretched himself out as he exclaimed: 'How wonderful to be drunk by the Faceless One, to make Him drunk with our own dreams! How beautiful that, alone in the middle of the fields, we can offer ourselves to His thirst!'"

After saying this, Rabbi Alessandro Luzzato took out a bottle of wine and glasses, and offered his bewildered visitor a drink.

"*Leḥayim!*", he said raising his voice. "To life!"

"To life," Zevi answered.

"Remember," added the master after tasting the wine, "that being alone reveals what is behind the folds of the heart: strands of light reaching towards heaven, twinkling stars in the aortic arch."

Alone, in Hebrew lebad לבד, *combines two concepts:* leb לב, *heart, and* bad בד, *a piece of cloth, but also a vein or artery. Numerically, alone or* lebad *equals 36, being thus equivalent to* Eloah אלה, *one of the names of the Creator, which once alliterated can be read as a dwelling, tent,* ohel אהל. *According to Biblical lore, the heart is the dwelling place and sanctuary of divinity* par excellence.

In the Cemetery

With a slow, ceremonious pace, four of the disciples of Rabbi Moshe Isfahani walked the yellow dust of Pir Bakan's cemetery in order to lay their memorial stones on his basalt tomb. Far away, the mountains had a salmon colour.

The sky was so blue it seemed like living lacquer, running sapphire.

"Do you remember what he told us the last day of his life?" asked Yoel of Balkh.

"I do," avowed Haim of Ghazni.

"It was a hot day," added Shaul of Shiraz.

"Swallows were flying around, and watching them from his deathbed," carried on Gad of Hamadan, "watching them fly beyond the window, he raised his voice, enfeebled by pain: 'When there is no master to guide the way, birds know only a tiny parcel of heaven and earth. But if they have a guide, even by night they can read the maps of the stars, and far in the distance they can catch sight of the eaves under which their fledglings will sleep. When a master of the flight leaves, it seems as if there is no frame or direction in our own wings, but soon enough a new swallow comes to take his place, and once more it is possible to return again and again to where you have been.'"

"That is what he said," confirmed Yoel of Balkh sadly.

"It was a hot day," repeated Haim of Ghazni.

"Hotter than today," said Shaul of Shiraz as he placed a small stone over the grave of Rabbi Moshe Isfahani.

"It is curious," observed Gad of Hamadan, whose prodigious memory they all trusted, "how he also used to say that a good master embodies what all his different disciples have in common, while a good disciple discovers what all beings have in common."

One swallow went by, then another. After a while the first star shone, and later the moon, the rugged mirror of the sun.

The swallow, dror דרור, *was both during the Biblical and post-Biblical periods a good example of the respect and responsibility existing between one generation,* dor דור, *and the next. You can return to the place from where you once departed if you carefully listen to the voice of your ancestors. In Ancient Egypt, the swallow (Hirundo rustica) was the ornithological embodiment of Isis, the goddess charged with "gathering" the dissevered parts of the body of her husband and brother Osiris.*

The Two Kinds of Master

"There are two kinds of wise words," said the singer of the Bremen synagogue, Rabbi Baruch Dreiser, a well known Talmud exegete and a jeweller dealing in semi-precious stones—those resembling stones that ripple, and those resembling the diamond.

A deep silence followed. Autumn had arrived with its mild white wines, and with slow and cold rains. That week's *haftarah* included the passage mentioning Moses' Law of Fire, brought to his people as mentioned in Deuteronomy 33:2.

"Some come from those masters who go to and fro, allowing themselves to follow the fancy of the time, charming and simple in their manners," he continued, "yet slightly raw when first met personally, fickle and unpredictable in their character. It is not necessary to come to them, for they are always there where we happen to be, around every river or stream, by the very gates of the city. Those who utter diamantine words, instead, who make use of eloquent and pithy turns of phrase, those are much harder to find, and it is almost always necessary to set out looking for them. They yield to no pressure, and in their solitude they endure terrible trials, unheard of zeal, anonymous and remote darkness. They strive after a transparency that shall be ours one day if we are able to find them. Most pour their strength out following very precise laws: those of their own clarity."

The surrounding silence became still deeper. A chair creaked. The lamps were now giving off a delicate paraffin smell.

"The common stone builds up enclosures and fences, it raises walls and props up platforms," said Rabbi Baruch Dreiser. "The diamond gathers light and then radiates it; it is hard yet translucent, and even lying in the deepest pit, it will always be ready, even when unseen, to give testimony to the shining star. We are bound to live between these two teachings, notwithstanding the difficulty of building a diamantine shelter or transmuting the opacity of the water-worn rolling pebble into light. To live is to flow with the current; yet to be—this is to be born in the lowest and still give testimony to the highest."

The Sheet of Silence

Rabbi Abel Azulai of Casablanca had gone to France to study the most noble and prestigious career of architecture. Intelligent and studious, in less than twenty years he had secured everything a Jew can wish for: moral, popular and professional certainty. But when he was sixty, a wandering blind musician crossed his path, Baba Yehuda Sagi Nahor, who came from inland Morocco and played with unusual mastery the vielle, an instrument inherited from his Spanish ancestors, and which he used to accompany old Sephardic songs. Being used to his position of authority, to see all his projects through, Rabbi Azulai of Casablanca renounced for a while his will, and decided to follow the wandering musician after hearing from him this song:

> The house of the universe
> has a starry ceiling;
> why cover your head
> when rain is pure light?
> My blind eyes taught my ears
> the stellar song of silence.

"And this is how I became his disciple," he used to recall. "During the first year he asked everything about me; during the second one he had me learn by heart a passage from the Torah chosen at will; and in the third year he did what no man had ever been able to do to me: he silenced my mind. When one morning, as I kept him company on his market round, I asked him how he did it, he replied:

'Authentic silence, real silence, draws an invisible sheet between your feet and the floor, no matter where you stand. When you succeed in hearing it, in just a tiny fraction of time your weight decreases and you know more.'

'Is that the stellar song of silence?' I asked, remembering the song that had made me his disciple, and he said:

'No. This is letting your feet tread on non-intention, alighting like the dew, which comes in peace, and in peace evaporates.'"

Thanks to a meaningful coincidence, a stroll is in Hebrew ṭiyul טיול*, a word containing the name for dew,* ṭal טל*, whilst a sheet,* riquaʻ רקוע*, derives from the same root as* raqiaʻ רקיע*, meaning sky, firmament. The sheet alluded to by the blind musician is a sort of heavenly void made evident by deep silence, and rediscovered by well-directed attention, between the soles of our feet and the path we stand on.*

The Creator and His Creatures

Two Talmud and Torah students from Lodz got caught in a frightful argument about the limits between the Creator and His creatures. Rafael and Jacob were deep in the Polish forests on a meditation retreat, and absorbed as they were in their argument they failed to notice the arrival of Bronislaw Legnica. This puppeteer was famous throughout the Nysa region, where he regularly paid visits to the dead birch trees, looking for the wood he would use for his princes and princesses, ogres and blacksmiths, goblins and dragons.

"Hey Jews!" he interrupted upon hearing them argue, "You fight over trifles, and you can't hear the nightingale's call for the yet unripe cherries, nor do you smell the perfume of fresh sap, nor do you enjoy the song of the wind-blown leaves."

"Were you overhearing us?" Rafael asked, worried that he had been surprised in the middle of his verbal engrossment by such an extraordinary artist as Bronislaw Legnica.

"Of course I was."

"What is your opinion, then?" asked Jacob.

"Our sages hold that the Creator fills every place, *memaleh maqom* ממלא מקום, which implies He is in all His creatures, but also that He transcends them and exceeds them. What is the limit then, between Him and us? What is the frontier? How can He at the same time be and not be in the tongue I speak with and in these eyes I see you with?"

"Poor me," replied the puppeteer, "if I thought too much, if I used my head too much, my puppets' strings would all be tangled; every one of my characters would like to hang from the other's rod, and instead of making people laugh for what they represent, the public would mock their maker as a clumsy victim of his own doubts."

"And what do you do then," Rafael wanted to know, "to prevent such a thing from happening?"

"I let them be whatever each one of them tries to play: villains or noblemen, naughty or romantic, murderers or angels."

"Yes," insisted Jacob, "but you come here looking for wood to carve them, you conceive their faces and you design their clothes, you draw their noses and you round off their shoulders. You are like a little god for your creatures."

"That's what I used to think!" exclaimed Bronislaw Legnica, as he cut a branch off and smiled ironically. "Until I realised that each tree, as each button which serves as an eye, or each piece of cloth that will be part of a costume, they all choose their inclination, they already bespeak their character! Indeed, we are like God's clock cuckoo, but it is as likely He ignores both the hours of our pleasures and the hours of our sorrows, and He only knows about us that we are made of a wood too weak to emulate Him. When we think we are approaching His kingdom, like a pendulum we swing back, and when we think He goes far from us, He is actually preparing His return. Do not seek God above your own heads. Look downwards; remember his pendulum."

Jacob and Rafael, overwhelmed by the puppeteer's means of expression, watched him peel some branches, taking off the bark, and then light his pipe.

After a few unexpected minutes of silence in the midst of the spring forest, the man from Legnica carried on:

"Even though the wild cherry is bitter, the nightingale sings; even though the sap spills, the tree does not drain off. And the leaves, what are they spending their time on, but on sharpening their edges between the *aah*s of the wind and the *ooh*s of my admiration?"

The Eager Student

Isaac Hacohen of Soria welcomed in his studio Tobias of Guadalajara with the purpose of receiving him, on his own request, into the Garden of the Walnut, a vaguely-defined society, whose scattered members devoted themselves to the study and practice of the secret art of Kabbalah. After his first lessons, the young man was so eager and happy that he vented the following question:

"Do you think, Rabbi Isaac, that one day I will be able to learn the beautiful things you teach?"

"Perhaps," replied laconically the man from Soria while he dug around the emblematic walnut in his garden, a wide space where they had both come together for the twilight hour.

"Everything seems to me so huge, so fabulous, so incredible," continued Tobias of Guadalajara, "that I doubt my own abilities."

"You only have to repeat, like King David in his day: 'Open Thou mine eyes, that I may behold wondrous things out of Thy law.'"

"Is that enough? Will I be able? When, how and where to search?"

"I suppose so many questions must overpower you," said Isaac Hacohen.

"They do, by heaven they do."

Then Isaac Hacohen summoned from a nearby old tree a blackbird he was used to feeding, and once the bird was near enough, he asked young Tobias to silently put in the palm of his right hand all those questions he had. Bewildered at such a practice, the eager student was slow to react, but when he did, the master fashioned a garland of qualms with his recent disciple's queries, then offered them, together with some bread crumbs, to the bird, saying:

"Dispel in laughter the anxiety of this young man, and go tell the Creator that his eyelids are opening after his eyes."

"I am sorry, Master," smiled Tobias of Guadalajara. "That is impossible; the eyelids are always ahead of the pupils."

"You have seen the first wonder," observed Isaac Hacohen. "Next time you shall be fed by the blackbird's flight."

The passage quoted by Rabbi Isaac Hacohen of Soria comes from Psalm 119:18, and its original includes the word gal גל *for uncovering, opening, revealing, with the possible meaning of wave. Centuries have confirmed the existence of electromagnetic waves through which light shows us, instant after instant, the renewed miracles of the Creation mentioned by the Torah, a teaching in a language as cryptic as poetic. Once the eye learns to see, the vision can fearlessly wander off in the object of contemplation.*

Enlightenment and Return

Yoshiro Tamashi, a disciple of the renowned Japanese Hebraist Setsuzo Kotsuji, a descendant of Shinto priests and a meditation master of repute, came to the Alliance with the People of the Book under the name of Noah, Noah Tamashi, after studying the *Sefer Yetsirah* or *Book of the Formation*, for four years and two months, in the scented isolation of a Kyoto garden, and after coming to the conclusion that the universality of light is no less than the mystical experience of the lightning conveying it. Like an abacus of myriad combinations, the Torah had enabled him to sail through both time and the hyperspace of pain and ecstasy. This was a meagre relief, however, when you consider he came from a family who had perished under the radioactive ashes in Hiroshima. When he read in the *Yetsirah* the passage where it is affirmed that "ten numbers correspond to ten infinities: their perception is like unto the lightning, and they decidedly point towards the infinite," and when he went again, astonished, over its letters, two, three times, trembling like a leaf of rice-paper, the verses of Basho the poet came to his mouth:

> How admirable!
> To see lightning and not to think
> life is fleeting.

For the very same terrifying blaze begets countless suns and consumes forever an innocent piece of land. The same brightness precedes death and announces rebirth. Noah Tamashi looked at his hands, counted his fingers, and in a single wink he saw there those ten infinities of his enlightenment. It was then that he felt such a great love, such a huge compassion for all living beings, that he went to the frogs of a temple pond to croak to them his sighs and moans, his monosyllables and sobs of gratitude, since he had discovered that to be converted means to return to the point of departure.

When the green amphibians became silent, he understood that at that moment they had heard him.

The Sefer Yetsirah *or* Book of Formation *does indeed say in its second chapter that such is the character of supreme perception, thus suggesting to Kabbalah students that lightning is a dance between magnetic fields, the kiss between two worlds recognising each other, a crack through which the sky shows its real face of unlimited energy. Furthermore, given that numerically* ha-baraqah הברקה *(312), enlightenment, equals a return,* shib שיב *(312), whoever attains enlightenment returns thereby* to being wherever he is.

The Tear Phial

Due to an inguinal hernia with which he had come to the world, Lo-Yadua, the Unknown Rabbi, could not stand firmly on the ground during his early childhood. When a child knows pain before happiness, the unsteady before the steady, it takes longer than usual for his salty tears to become sweet. Thoughtful and loving, his mother had then the blessed idea to collect his tears in a glass perfume phial she placed under his eyelids every time the child, by now three years old, would cry, not for the hernia—as it had ceased to be there after the surgery—but for the memory of the still recent pain, letting out long-drawn, irrepressible sobs. Her task was not easy, though, as the little hands would flutter around trying to fend off what they thought might be some evil medical device they could never be rid of.

After blending the tears with kohl and powdered coal, the mother of the Unknown One said to him one day:

"Look how the most wonderful thing has happened: you have wept out all the darkness in your heart, and there are now almost no shadows left inside of you. Next time you cry, your tears will be clearer than the little stream we visit with your father."

By and by, and since she had stopped adding coal to the mixture, adding a touch of homemade perfume and some water, the mother could finally tell the child that something even more extraordinary was taking place.

"Your soul is starting to smell like a field of chamomile."

"What is chamomile, Mama?" Lo-Yadua asked.

"Come, I will show you."

They went out to the fields. They walked for a long while in silence. The first spring flowers made even more bountiful the green of the meadows.

"These are the chamomiles," the mother of the Unknown One said finally, "buttons of the sun on the robe of the earth."

More than forty years after this scene took place, the Unknown One was able to ascertain a surprising symmetry between the word tear, dim'ah דמעה, *and earth,* adamah אדמה, *both of which share three letters and differ in one: the* 'ain ע, *indeed, refers to the eye from which tears spring, and the* alef א *marks the divine trace left on earth. Our human pupil thinks it suffers on account of a limit that the earth, amused and untiring, keeps expanding at every new turn.*

The Mandrake, the Saint and the Retarded Son

There lived, on the outskirts of Baghdad, a cobbler who had a retarded son called Isaac Iḥur, the usual target of spoofs and the occasional prank, and who every summer would be found chasing blue butterflies across the fields. Worried about what his son's destiny would be after his death, the father was keen to visit every physician or healer who came to town, trying to find a cure for his affliction. The mother being dead, with no siblings, it seemed to the old man that the Creator's protection would not be enough to keep Isaac once he left the kingdom of the living.

A saint by the name Abu Niflaot went by the Jewish cobbler's shop loudly crying:

"Buy the miraculous plant, the mandrake that cures the love spell, awakens dormant powers, heals the phthisic and restores the cripple, strengthens the only eye of the one-eyed and raises to its highest Aaron's rod!"

The cobbler came out running over nails and soles from his shack, spilling a glue jar and tripping over a cord. Followed closely by his son Isaac, he paid an enormous sum for the mandrake. That night, after duly grinding it, he boiled it and, upon the saint's advice, gave the concoction to his retarded son to drink on a cloudless morning. Two weeks after, by the dry bed of a river, Isaac found a plum branch which had served as a shepherd's staff, and he took it home thinking this was the rod meant by Abu Niflaot, which would rise to its highest.

The following week it was all covered in flowers. Afterwards came the leaves, and not a full month had passed when the branch-staff was already flaunting the green roundness of four beautiful plums for everyone to see. This prodigy came to the ears of the saint, who paid an inquisitive visit to the cobbler's. But in spite of the green and wondrous fruits, the retarded boy was just like before; his father did not understand a thing of what was happening, and Isaac kept being late everywhere, tripping over his own steps, or falling asleep standing during religious services.

They decided to hang the amazing branch from the ceiling of the shop so that everybody could see the miracle. The wandering healer, not wasting a single minute in philosophies or trifles, went to an orchard where he cut ten, fifteen branches, and lying about their origin, he claimed to have soaked them in copious amounts of mandrake water, and promised them to be just about to display their gifts. Naturally, after he had made his money he left. One day after, the entire region was shaken by an earthquake, and the whole town fell to the ground with the exception of the shoe shop, propped by the miraculous staff and by the work of Isaac, who had started singing, while he scraped some leather pieces:

> Sooner or later it is the same,
> the branch I found made haste,
> the ground we tread is so alive
> both in the dry as in the wet.
> Sooner or later it is the same,
> man is no tree,
> the ground is no tomb,
> the breeze speaks without hands.

With the years, the weather, rain and winds, the staff became a lush tree which outlasted the four walls of the shop and the cobbler himself. A tree under which Isaac the retarded, who had learnt to sigh with glee, would teach the youth in search of a beloved how to measure the intake and release of the breath of love. And when they asked him why he did that, he would proudly reply:

"My father used to cover feet; I instead uncover the softest path for the longest steps."

Everywhere slowness is found, say the sages, either wilful or unintentional, such delay in both small and great matters is a good adviser, for it allows us to ponder the depth of their destiny. Isaac's nickname, iḥur אחור, *delay, contains for us a light,* or אור, *a kindred feeling,* aḥ אח, *or the very breath of the Spirit,* ruaḥ רוח.

Noah's Fate

"Of all possible fates," Rabbi Nehemiah of Aleppo used to say, "of all the gifts from the Creator to the sons of His people, if I could choose, I would prefer the noble fate of Noah."

He was a trader in incense and sandalwood oil, rose essence and balsam. He had ten sons and one daughter, and on summer nights he would sleep alone on his veranda, rambling about star names, some of which he had learnt by heart from an Iraqi merchant, without even knowing their position: Mirah, Al-Amaq, Al-Kanib, Al-Firaz. He had built for himself a miniature ark he filled with ladybirds, worms and shiny beetles, thus coming closer to his favourite Biblical character.

"Abraham our Father," he observed, "abandoned everything in order to create everything. Moses traversed the fiery valley of the Law, and he forged statutes with its sparks. Joshua conquered Jericho, Ezekiel dreamt the temple's proportions, Jeremiah saw an almond branch and he heard the voice of the Maker, but Noah—oh, Noah was a friend of animals and plants, he preserved love and the relations between species. He read on the rainbow the pact with the living, and he knew the joys and dreams of wine."

"But you are unable," his friends would tease him, "to tell a goat from an antelope. In the case of a new flood, you wouldn't have saved a single hen."

Rabbi Nehemiah of Aleppo had to wait months before he saw what he had asked from heaven: a rain so strong it half flooded the lower ground of his house. Then he climbed up to the veranda with the best of his hens, laughing out heartily while his people drained the kitchen and the bedrooms, while they cleared the mud and they swore and complained at the unruly weather. Later on, when the sun showed again, he shouted at them from upstairs:

"I have not only saved my hen, but it has even laid an egg between my hands. Not even Noah was so lucky!"

Beneath Every Human Being

Rabbi Ezekiel of Bucharest used to quote the following passage from Exodus, 25:8: "And let them make me a sanctuary; that I may dwell among them,"[1] in order to illustrate, in his lessons, the pre-eminence of the human above the inert, of the living above all architecture, of the subject above the object.

"After all," he would insist, "how shall we understand that *tokham* תוכם, 'beneath them', if not as referring to that which we tread upon any minute of our lives, the place where our shadow ends and our light begins, or perhaps, under our skin, like that which throbs between veins and arteries bearing witness to His Divine Presence amongst us?"

"It could be," intervened a student named Samuel Gordon, from Jassy in Moldavia, "it could be that 'beneath' did not simply mean within or inside, but also *between*, in which case the Creator would be dwelling between us if we all make a common place for His silence, a little space for His utmost greatness."

"Should the master allow me," cut in Amos of Ploiesti, the marriage contract scribe, "there was no temple at the time of Exodus; the Tabernacle would change abode with the children of Israel, and the dynamic was then more important than the static. This is why the Torah emphasises personal factors above temple configuration."

"On the other hand, the mention of *them*," continued Samuel Gordon, "suggests that every rite is collective, and that its efficacy

---

[1] An alternative and more literal translation for the final part of this passage would be "dwell beneath them", since the phrasal preposition *be-tokham* בתוכם is centred on *tokh* תוך, meaning both *under* and *among*.

is void if the celebration does not penetrate each and every participant."

It was a September day, and Rabbi Ezekiel of Bucharest was travelling with his friends and disciples towards Constanza in order to supervise the arrival of a shipment of citrons for the Feast of Booths. This shipment, coming from Jaffa, had travelled thousands of miles, always through Jewish hands, in order to furnish the small scattered communities with the four sacred species indispensable for the feast: willow, myrtle, palm and citron.

Rabbi Ezekiel stopped suddenly, bent to the ground, and taking a patch of dry moss from between the feet of Amos of Ploiesti, he said:

"Give me the water jug."

It did not take long for the dry plant to revive upon exposure to some liquid, nor to pass from a withered brownish colour to lemon green within a few minutes of curiosity and expectation.

"Can you see? Beneath all of us," observed Rabbi Ezekiel, "there is always some dry moss, some charred bunch of herbs, a withered branch; but it is enough for a drop, a tear or a shiver of emotion to move us, precise and fresh, touching us in the right spot, for us to feel as if we are building the sanctuary, the sanctuary of the way, the tabernacle of our travels around the world."

> *The fact that a little alliteration can make moss,* taḥab טחב*, into* beṭaḥ בטח*, meaning trust and certainty, shows to what extent a true master is a decoder of circumstance, someone who establishes harmony between the outside and the inside for everyone to see and for everyone's benefit.*

The Desert and the Verb

"Until you are completely by yourselves with the beating of your heart," Rabbi Yosef Kolonimos of Hamburg used to say, "by yourselves with your sighs, in the middle of your despair's wasteland, or at the crossroads of your grief and pain; sunk down in the cruellest hopelessness, in the dullest indifference; stifled by the most intense of lamentations; harassed by all your failures, and surrounded by the corpses of your unfulfilled wishes; until what is lowest on earth does not equal the abyss of your lowliness, and until the end presses upon you like just a beginning; forever far removed from any control, yearning and every opportunity for mastery; until then no living word, mark my words, shall nourish and be a remedy to you."

The desert, real or imaginary, is the best of grammarians and the most unfailing of poets.

If it came to happen that one of his pupils, enraptured by his master's fiery eloquence, would let out a tear, thereby indicating that *he was that sad character*, Yosef Kolonimos, upon noticing, would calmly come to him, and placing an almost transparent hand on his shoulder, would continue:

"And then, when the newly found verb has become yours, as yours as your skin's hue, your own and as untransferable as a rush of oxygen entering your lungs; once you and that word are made of the same extraordinary substance, a mixture of pollen and fire, of pure water and thunder, lily and iron, then you shall have to return to the place where those yet unborn abide, those who know nothing about themselves, and even less about the spiritual dimension of stars, in order to gift them with your verb, as someone who upon the thresholds leaves food for the birds, stooping at their closed doors and leaving before they are fully opened."

Thus spoke Rabbi Yosef Kolonimos of Hamburg, candlemaker and occasional baker.

During the Biblical period, prophets and their sons, called bnei nevi'im, *would go down to the Dead Sea for their solitary meditation practices. Considering that desert is in Hebrew* midbar מדבר, *and verb, or word, is* dabar דבר, *the fact that the letter* mem מ, *distinguishing these terms, indicates provenance or origin, explains somehow those excursions into the dry loneliness of the Judaean desert searching for psychic transmutations. Besides, given that the numeric value of* dabar (206) *matches that of the verb* ra'ah (206), *to see, to watch, to glimpse, it is no wonder that such spiritual exercises would transform the prophets into genuine seers.*

The Cartographer and the Orange Blossom

Yehuda Cresques of Majorca, the cartographer, went for a walk by the seaside in order to lighten his mind and relieve his hands. The weather was hot, the sea was warm, and its endless music was more pleasing to his ears than the contempt of the envious and the chit-chat of fools. There was an orange grove near his house. It belonged to Deborah Azadel, a pretty brunette girl he often used to hear singing:

> Swift bird
> answer me:
> Where have you been today?
> All night
> my restless eyelids spent
> without a taste of sleep.

Were these Halevi verses, Ibn Gabirol's, or perhaps Umm Hanna's, the daughter of Granada's *qadi*, Abu Muhammad Abd al-Haqq ibn 'Atiya, whose fame and deeds had reached the island?

"Master," she said, offering upon his approach an orange flower, "do not strain your eyes on the lines of so many maps. The earth is abloom; the heavens smile. The sea has forged, for the sun's wedding, rings of light in the breaking foam."

Yehuda Cresques smiled as he received the gift, and for a long while kept walking imbued in the citrous scent of the garden. This flower, the orange blossom, symbolising love and devoted couples, foretelling with its leaves vague promises or thwarted destinies, used to intrigue him time after time. No wonder man can come to think, he said to himself, that when he embraces his beloved he is touching the land of his dreams. But for that to be real, he will yet have to try his courage against earthquakes and droughts, his patience with litigations of space and limits, and his serenity in the face of the conceding of rights or turns of humour. Being a cartographer he knew well that one should not mistake maps for terrain, projects with their execution.

"After all," he muttered, letting his feet sink in the sea, "what is a symbol if it does not flow, or a maritime chart if we dare not travel? And what is love if we ignore the sway of its waves?"

One of the Hebrew words for symbol is remez רמז, *and Mediaeval cartographers like our Jewish-Majorcan Yehuda Cresques made ample use of them as they filled their maps with griffins, leviathans, the jaws of monsters, enormous whirlpools, wind roses and more. This showed that travelling across land or sea not only depended on one's skills or on the weather's changing fortunes, but also on companions on the route. The vitality of a symbol, following Cresques' thought, will depend on* remez רמז *preserving at every moment its quality of* zerem זרם, *flowing, natural current, so that we may reach the shore of our designs. Otherwise their very form veils the meaning they are intended to convey.*

The Dot and the Line

The young student Mordechai of Prague came to pay a visit to the well-known rabbi and geometer Hillel of Vienna, to whom he had addressed a letter querying him on a mention of the *teli*, or dragon, found in the *Book of Formation* or *Sefer Yetsirah*. Of the three principles mentioned in the 13th century *Book of Brightness* or *Bahir*, namely the celestial dragon, the Zodiac circle and the human heart—three levels interrelated in such a way that there is a dragon in the heart, a heart in the Zodiac and a Zodiac circle in the mythical beast—this image of the dragon was in his judgment the hardest to understand.

"I can clearly see, master," said Mordechai to Hillel the geometer, "that the Zodiac or wheel of life causes our months and seasons, and that it projects its symbols over our heavenly rhythm; and I can also see clearly that the *tsimtsum*, creation, the expansion and contraction of the cosmos, is echoed in every single one of our human heartbeats; but when it comes to the dragon..."

"According to some Kabbalah masters," answered Rabbi Hillel as he turned an 18th century armillary sphere reproducing the movements of the sky, "*teli* or the dragon would be the imaginary axis around which the skies revolve. It is supposed to be a fantastic line from which hangs the heavenly sphere, like an orange from its tree or a fuchsia from a branch. However, I think the dragon is that scaly, reptilian bridge extended between our principles and our actions or, if you prefer, between the letters *yod* and *vav*, the dot and the line, Father and Son. The head is the fruit of our body's tree: should it hang too low, any passer-by could pluck it. If on the other hand it is buried deep amongst the branches, the sun will never ripen it; and should it happen that its leaf stalk is weak, no sap coming from the heart would give it the glow it deserves and awaits."

"What if the head grows too high?"

"Blackbirds will peck it and gales will bite at it. It will inadvertently take its position for maturity and its pride for wisdom."

They were slowly sipping their afternoon tea, and beyond the window-panes of the geometer's studio you could see spring sneaking away between lush chestnuts and broad oaks.

"We have an astronomical confirmation for the Zodiac, and an anatomical confirmation for the heart," said the master, "but about their relations, synchronies, conflicts, that is, about the dragon, we know little or nothing. If you prolong the letter *yod* downwards, the Father becomes Son, the principle action, the brainstem and spinal cord. From the divine, or rather, from the secret to the revealed, there is an expansion, but from the human back to the divine there is a path of synthesis, contraction after contraction, since the *vav*, in order to become *yod* again, must perforce shrink, grow smaller."

"But then," continued young Mordechai of Prague, "is there a number, some concept that protects us along that journey from heart to head, from the sensible to the intelligible?"

"If you chance upon the door," replied the master, "and sometimes that door is a simple word, a syllable, a knock, a sunrise, an embrace, a fall, a spark, a taste, a flash, a death, a dream; if you chance upon that door, the dragon will lift its wings for you to see the treasure they were covering."

"And what is that treasure?"

"The one about which it is said in Exodus 19:5: 'you shall be a special treasure to Me.'"

"I don't follow you."

The master stood up, set in motion the armillary sphere, and taking a mirror confronted Mordechai of Prague with it.

"Look at yourself: He is your treasure if you are His key."

Mario Satz

Within the oral tradition or Kabbalah, it is not uncommon for the Tetragrammaton to be written vertically: י ה ו ה *presumably to highlight the likeness between the Creator and Adam Kadmon or Archetypal Man. In that case, the letter yod* י *would stand for our head, while vav* ו *would symbolise both the spine and the heart axis. Besides, from the numerical point of view, the difference between these letters amounts to four (*י*=10,* ו*=6), whose alphabetic character is* dalet *and whose symbol is the door, hence the master's mention of it. At the same time, the Biblical passage hinges on an emblematic term,* li לי, *to me, a word where we can see outlined, behind the directional factor of the lamed* ל, *the yod* י *of the Creator, the basic dot from which all lines are made. Now if we add to this* li לי, *to me, one more letter, namely the tau* ת, *representing the world, the earth, the visible universe, it turns out that we will have tamed the dragon,* teli תלי, *at the same time we acknowledge that the universe is his, since he is in fact the universe itself.*

Light from the Air

Every morning as he got up, Schmuel the Bark Gatherer, admirer of Baal Shem Tob, whom he had seen healing children and elder people, would come out of his hut, were it winter or summer, under snow, or rain, or shiny sun, and he would say aloud:

"Light from the air, light from the air: let every point of the world hold for me the entire world."

After that, carrying his little polished axe, he would plunge into the Carpathian forest around his village, with a huge sack upon his shoulders and the round flask in which he collected birch sap. Schmuel would pull the barks apart, then sort them according to their humidity and colours, while he hummed tunes whose origins were unknown to him. This melodious habit had earned him the friendship of birds and bees. The few letters he had learned were barely enough for him to spell his full name on ruled paper.

In spite of eating like a lion, he was slimmer than an Egyptian bas-relief, and so stealthy in his comings and goings that you would hear the thump of the bark sack on the ground before noticing his own footsteps approaching. In those days, poor people would boil and eat the tender barks, and shoemakers would use them to make flimsy summer sandals. Also in those days, whoever could would leave for America, looking for wider skies and more extended lands, far from the Cossacks' reach and from disdainful noblemen. But since Schmuel had many children to cater for, few lights and practically no ambition, he would just ask of each of his daily movements to take him to a humble plenitude. This is why he repeated:

"Light from the air, light from the air: let every point of the world hold for me the entire world."

Once, upon hearing him, Rabbi Mendel came back home with tears in his eyes, for he had just verified through the mouth of a simpleton that for which most sagacious minds never cease striving: for what is in front of their eyes to become a revealed vision.

In Genesis 3:8 we can read: "And they heard the voice of the Creator walking in the garden at the air of the day." Rabbi Mendel could not help recalling this passage once he had heard the words of the Bark Gatherer, evoking the fact that for the Kabbalah it is the air, avir אויר, *which acts as a vehicle for light, or* אור, *stirring it into motion with the diamantine power of the tiniest of sacred letters,* yod י.

Perfect Ear and Imperfect I

Nathan of Kuopio, whose family was originally from Leningrad, used to be an entomologist before he took to studying the secrets and beauties of the Torah. He came to have such a knowledge of his country's lakes, that locals would ask him about weather movements upon his return from field trips, knowing that Nathan would have seen before anyone else had, reflected in the mirrors of the water, the first glimpses of brewing storms and the delicate early signs of oncoming spring. The habit of ground level attention and the lonely practice of silence had sharpened his ear so much that Nathan could make out a middle scale C sharp in the passing flight of a buzzing bee. Water insects over and around the lakes during the summer produced, according to him, a rather dull F sound. He went as far as ascertaining that the higher pitched the note emitted by recently fed mosquitoes, the hotter the day would be. Thirty metres away from their nest, he could tell the oriole chicks were complaining for lack of food; he knew the differences between the bumblebee's thorough bass and the lower notes of a double bass. Whenever a kingfisher plunged, Nathan of Kuopio knew, without any need to look, whether it had been successful or not. His hearing was so remarkable that, like with oriental monks, his earlobes grew very long, to the point that his disciples, once he had become a rabbi, used to call him Oznei Sheket, Ears of Silence.

In spite of such a marvellous auditory faculty, it happened that whenever he was absorbed in his studio, or lost in his vague meditations, Nathan of Kuopio would very seldom hear when he was being called. Were it his wife, or one of his children, or were it that a disciple or another master needed his attention, he would always take long to respond. And when he did, he seemed so absentminded that more often than not he would need to have questions repeated.

"His capacity of abstraction became greater than his capacity of attention," said his closest disciple upon Nathan's death.

"I don't think so," replied Rabbi Adam of Vaasa. "In him we could simply see verified the saying attributed to Rabbi Meir Hamishpat of Girona: 'Whoever hears the delights and wonders of the world is deaf to his own name.'"

During the Talmudic period, the existence of the sagi nahor סגי נהור, *the "blind through excess of light", became proverbial; in a similar way, the greatest of those who attend to the wisdom of the Torah are often referred to as* oznei sheqet אוזני שקט, *"hearers or listeners of silence". Because of the gematric equivalence between silence,* sheqet שקט *(800), and root,* shoresh שורש *(800), they say that only he who is silent on the surface will understand in depth.*

The Carob Tree Water Carrier

Up in Northern Greece there lived a man known from childhood to Rabbi Hanan Mariasis because he had been a patient of his father, the physician Rabbi Moshe Mariasis of Abdera. As a young man, this patient had worked as a shoeshine boy for the Turkish army, where he had had no end of miseries at the hands of the Ottoman officers. He used to come to his health checks carrying an old dark leather goatskin he would never part with, not even when he disrobed for examinations. Out of discretion, out of consideration to his age and his venerable white moustache, the doctor would let him be, thinking it was a mere childish habit he had not given up entirely. But one day the son, less tactful than his father, queried him:

"What do you have, good man, in that old goatskin you never once leave aside?"

Surprised by the question, the man, whose name was Yohanes, Yohanes Afitis, replied:

"You see, I grew up herding goats in a place full of carob trees. I ate from their sweet pods, I took shelter under their branches for fifteen years before I had to go reluctantly to serve the Turks. Now, in the courtyard of the barracks where they forced me to work there happened to be a huge and lonely carob tree. The soldiers were in the habit of plucking its branches to feed their night fires, and one after the other, stick by stick, they used its wood until in a few years they left it utterly wasted, like a dark, rugged and sad skeleton. One day, as I walked past, the carob tree told me: 'I am thirsty, give me water; I am thirsty, give me life.'"

Rabbi Hanan Mariasis, bewildered, stared at the water carrier, noticing the strength with which his tough hands held the goatskin, and he turned to look at his father, who stood with a very serious air at the entrance of the surgery.

"You see, my boy," said Yohanes to Rabbi Hanan, who was no more than a child then. "Water was so severely rationed that we servants were made to die with thirst. So I took the few seeds left on the poor abused old tree, and I swore to myself I would keep them always wet. They are in here: listen."

He shook the goatskin, and a rattle was heard, a whisper of little bells, dull and faint; the voice of the old seeds.

The water carrier let out a smile, and with a gesture of assured momentousness he added:

"At last, when they let me go, I returned to my land, went back with the carobs. Since then I water them every day, even when it rains. I still wonder if the one who spoke to me did so because it could not bear any more, because the pain it endured was so intense as to force out a cry of help. Let me tell you something, little one, and do not forget it: two equal sufferings are needed in order to grant a reunion in infinity. One is not enough."

The word carat, used to value the quality of gold and diamonds, derives from the constant weight of the little karat, *or Arabian carob seed, employed as a unit of measure in jewellery from a remote time. Its Hebrew equivalent is the term* ḥarub חרוב, *which slightly alliterated can be read as* be-ruaḥ ברוח, *in the Spirit, or through the Spirit. Everything that happens, whether we know it or not, has more than one reading, and behind every abstract fact there is usually, and originally, a sensible reality.*

When Facing Doubt, Trust the Work of the Universe

Many people came to visit Abu Salish of Marrakesh, in whose shop were sold the finest Persian rugs, Chinese silk tapestries, and bird and fruit-pattern embroidered wedding belts from Pakistan. Even though an insidious diabetes had made him all but blind, Abu Salish, who had in his childhood learnt by heart entire passages of the *Zohar*, used to rhythmically spell out loud Biblical verses, turning them over a hundred times, and commenting on them from all angles—upside down, downside up, from back to front, and from the inside out. Each time someone asked why he would make the same interpretation again, or why he would return to the same sentences, he would answer with an ironic smile:

"What matters is the point of view, the angle of observation. The earth avails itself of seasons to make its colours known, but beneath its bones, the rock stays equal to itself. What changes is called freedom; what remains is called constancy. If we are constant in spite of change, and if moreover we change with constancy, there is nothing we are not equal to."

His youngest grandson poured tea in tiny goblets which made music when the little spoons stirred the sugar, and afterwards, if he was not too tired, with the remaining quarter or less of his full vision, Abu Salish, the albino Jew, would read the destiny of his guests in the minuscule tea strands left at the bottom of the glasses. In his youth, as a tradesman, he had travelled much, crossing deserts and seas; but when he discovered the silence rising from a pile of a hundred or two hundred rugs together, he understood that that was his place: a shop filled with woven wools simulating Paradise, or cotton gardens so tiny and flexible as to fit in the handkerchief that holds a sneeze.

"When facing doubt," went one of his favourite sayings, "trust the work of the universe. Let him be the one who achieves what you can not achieve."

"Is perchance the universe a someone?" his grandson once asked him.

"In any case, it is not simply a 'what'," replied Abu Salish.

The Hebrew preposition but, abal אבל, *contains, when read with a different vocalisation,* ebel, *a duel, an affliction, a loss. We have thus the affirmation of a certain conditionality and a certain logic in the cosmic activity, since the mechanism of a given reasoning is introduced. Nevertheless, if we turn the word further and read it as* le-ab לאב, *for the father, or to God, then there is surrender, acceptance of the unknown and unconditional.*

Divine Presence

On the island of Djerba, Tunisia, among the cushions and wooden benches of the old synagogue, three disciples of Rabbi David Chambi, wrapped in the scent of mint and seashore murmurs, were discussing the meaning of the Shekhinah or Divine Presence.

"I can't remember any passage in the Torah where it is explicitly mentioned," said Moshe of Nefta.

"It is said to have hovered above the Tabernacle during the entire Exodus," remarked Abu Israel of Bizerta very seriously.

"As far as I understand, the Shekhinah is a sort of 'shadow of light', following the facts in the same manner as our shadow is a projection of our body," added Rabbi Azulai of Gabès.

None of them, however, appeared to be sure about what he said, since the ambiguity of the immanent is elusive as well as limited. Ibn Ezra, Maimonides and the masters of Islam had spoken about how, and from immemorial times, the infinite was reflected on the finite, but it was somehow easier to define what is vast and sublime than what belongs to the moment and daily life.

"They also say," continued Moshe of Nefta, "that the Shekhinah is the *kehilah* or the community of Israel itself whenever it invokes and incarnates the Creator. It will adopt the measure of the one experiencing it."

"This makes me right," said Rabbi Azulai of Gabès, "since in the same way that each body has its own shadow, every person has his or her share of divine radiance in their entrails."

The mint fragrance became stronger as the leaves were soaked in the hot tea. It would soon be dark over the sea, and the seagulls would continue their weightless flight through the air currents.

"Our master, Rabbi David Chambi," said Abu Israel of Bizerta, "used to belittle the importance of this kind of conversation. Do you remember? He often said that thinking on the effects of the Creator upon His Creation would paralyse the creature."

"And he also said," intervened Rabbi Azulai, "that it is in language where He is best revealed to us, His students, in the language that recounts His adventures in the memory of the human race."

"It is true," smiled Moshe of Nefta while relaxing. "I had forgotten: *shekhinah hi ha-safah*, the Divine Presence lives and manifests itself in the Hebrew letters."

The dusk found them reading and commenting on the passage from the Song of Solomon 2:13, where it is said: "Arise, my love, my beautiful one, and come away."

Both Shekhinah שכינה*, or Divine Presence, and* safah שפה*, tongue, language, add up to 385, this being the reason why many Kabbalists hold that divine immanence is, above all, a linguistic fact. In doing so, they are not oblivious to the fact that every written sign, every* ot אות*, being of feminine gender like* Shekhinah*, is in reality a womb of meaning or mother-letter.*

The Onion and the Value of Symbols

"You hold," remarked Rabbi Haim Vega Hacohen of Safed to his master, a faithful follower of the teachings of the Ari, Rabbi Menashe Albatel, "you hold that the entire Torah is a symbol which cannot be explained literally, and that it thus changes with every new reading, that it expands, branches out, spreads without thereby losing sight of its departure point."

Swaying under the spring breeze, vine leaves would off and on scrape their greenery against the white-washed wall of the synagogue courtyard. The sky looked like a lake surrounded by light from all quarters, and the deep earth a basket full of wonders.

"And so it is: words obey a bilateral symmetry, like your arms or legs; but symbols obey a radial symmetry, much like stars, which radiate from a centre in all directions."

"But the Torah," observed young Rabbi Amos Kaplan, "is woven with words, but does not seem to abound in symbols."

"You are wrong," Rabbi Menashe Albatel immediately replied. "Mount Sinai is a symbol, the Tabernacle yet another, as are also the twelve precious stones on the pectoral worn by the high priest."

"I am sorry, but I do not understand well how it is that an object, an event or a particular place," insisted Haim Vega of Safed, the only one who had been born in the holy city, "all things alluded to by words, how it is that they acquire the status of a symbol."

"Every word," explained Menashe Albatel, "comes from a preceding one and goes on to a third one, but symbols are like onions: they grow in the dark, and as you peel them, they reveal more and more layers, and this in such a way that force lines, subtle structural lines you see on each level, are reflected on each new layer. This is why, if you understand properly the play of allusions, you will obtain, as with the onion, a nourishment of multiple uses. Words are, in general, two-dimensional; symbols are polyphonic."

A bottle of Carmel wine was produced and the master poured a little in each glass.

"Let us drink to the onion," said Menashe Albatel smiling, "that from its tasty shade it may lead us to the enlightened contentment of the heart."

The Hebrew word for onion, batsal בצל, *can indeed be read also as* tsel צל, shade, *and* leb לב, heart. Curiously enough, it is said that the onion *(Allium cepa), an edible bulb in the Liliaceae family, acts as an excellent cardiac tonic.*

The Ear of Cereal

On the outskirts of Safed, where the slope of the Galilean mountains would allow it, like in the times of the Second temple, Kabbalists of the brotherhood of the Sacred Lion, Rabbi Luria, used to bury their dead in caves dug with diligence and care, deep enough to enable those who had been study companions in life to exercise their otherworldly dialogues upon the transparency of this or that verset. After introducing the corpses wrapped in their prayer shawls inside fragrant pine wood coffins, their next of kin and friends would throw wheat or barley seeds over the bare floor, at times singing the *nigun*, or the favourite tune of the deceased, or occasionally reciting the *Shema Israel* with swift, dry lips.

Rabbi Natan Algazel of Casablanca, who resided in Safed since the 1492 expulsion, wiped his tears as he left the cave where the remains of Rabbi Israel, dubbed the Ear of Cereal, had just been lain, and remarked:

"Every day of his life he was sitting at the bottom of his heart, attentive and happy before the Throne of the Most High, letting the ends of the *shabat* reach into every nook and cranny of his profane life."

The nearby mountain was ablaze with chirping birds, more and more unclouded with every twitter. It would soon be Easter. The Sultan's armies moved to and fro under their red turbans. Poverty among Safed's Jews was as common as a patch of grass on the edge of a cliff.

"I would like to know," remarked young Rabbi Amos Vital somewhat sadly, "why he was called the Ear of Cereal."

"Ah," smiled Rabbi Natan Algazel tenderly, "just as other people finger their amber rosaries or play with a clock as they study, Rabbi Israel would hold a ripe ear of cereal which he used to move as deftly as a draftsman his pen. He would as easily use it to scratch his beard, as to rub his forehead saying: 'Lord of the Universe, *boreh olamim,* Creator of the Worlds, fill my head with good thoughts and even better deeds. Grant my mind the endless fertility of the earth and the marvellous display of the heavens, and make unknown to me, I beg You, two of the saddest futilities of the soul: boredom and indifference.'"

The ear of cereal, or shibolet שבלת*, does indeed contain the heart,* leb לב*, of the thirty-two paths of wisdom, and the root* sat שת*, meaning a base or foundation. It is, however, also possible to read it, after a slight alliteration, as* le-Shabbat לשבת*, for the Shabbat or to the Shabbat, an expression which can in turn, through a mere change in the vocalisation, be made into* lashebet לשבת*, to sit down.*

His Soul Blossomed

Every time one of his disciples died, or arrived suddenly at the understanding of a difficult verse of Ecclesiastes—his favourite book of the Bible—the legendary and already elderly Rabbi Abraham Kalan of Singapore would say in Hebrew: *paraḥah neshmato* פרחה נשמתו, his soul blossomed.

Being asked why death and profound understanding were in his eyes identical would usually take him over the darkest passages of history, a discipline whose study had earned him a doctorate at Oxford. He used to recall, for instance, that Greeks of the Classical period gave initiation in their Eleusinian mysteries the name of *teleute*, to cease, to die; and that among Kabbalists there was no access to *tam* תם, the perfect, without going through its opposite, or *met* מת, death, what is dead. Other times he would hold that Yama, the Hindu god of the deceased, gave rise to the Sanskrit verb *yam*, to offer, to tame, or to transform, to convert, whence the difficulty, if not the impossibility, of living every instant as it arises anew, that is, unless you become capable of dying at every instant that passes.

"I can accept that," his friend Rabbi Yosef Sinlan of Malacca sighed one day, "but I frankly do not understand why you should use the verb 'to blossom' before the very gates of death and understanding. Is the soul perchance born when it dies? And do plants know what they are only after they have blossomed?"

"Let us take one verse," said Rabbi Abraham Kalan of Singapore, "let us say, for instance, Ecclesiastes 3:19: 'they have all one breath.' The word 'all', *lekol*, in this phrase has the same numerical value as *va-ed*, for ever, eternally, and this gives us the idea of the immortality of cosmic life, the life of species that transform into one another. When young Rabbi Saul of Baghdad came to see me, and I told him there was a message for him in that 'all', as there is one now for you, *lekha*, his eyelids broadened like jasmine petals under the first summer sun.

A smile then kindled Rabbi Yosef's face. He rose from his chair, and taking a few steps through the exotic garden of his host, he told himself that should he die at that moment, it would have been worth living until then, if only to live the previous scene. The master, in turn, plunged his flat nose into a large gardenia and half-closed his eyes. It was the evening, and yet it felt like day; it was a Tuesday, and yet it felt like Saturday.

The saying paraḥah neshmato פרחה נשמתו *alludes to expiring, dying, while at the same time pointing to the word* peraḥ פרח, *a flower. The quotation from* Ecclesiastes 3:19, *which contains the meaning-laden expression* lekol לכל *(80), numerically equals the eternal, the continuous,* va-ed ועד; *but it also includes* lekha לך, *for you, to you, showing that every one of us belongs to that "all" to which we are threaded even unawares.*

Blessing of the Moon

Whenever Nissim Ezekiel saw the crescent moon, he went to the seashore, and while the sky was still rosy with the last twilight glimmerings, he would say:
"Lovely Lady of Mother-of-Pearl, beautiful Mother of Jasmine, light hidden in our nails: no matter how far we go, do not forget us. Be for our memory like mint refreshing, kindle our passion; and cease not going around the navels of the women of Israel."

Not all the Jews in Konkan, Western India, saw the same wonders in the moon. Pearl and sponge fishers as they were, mother-of-pearl carvers and sitar luthiers, they were more interested in the success of their businesses than in what took place in the skies.

"May your dew be made of happy tears," repeated Nissim Ezekiel, who had studied some Hebrew in Bombay under Ephraim Baghdadi, "and may all our building help us unite and not be separated."

Like other romantics in the way of the Chinese poet Li Tai Po, Blue Lotus Flower, who drowned after singing to the moon's reflection, Nissim rowed into the sea on a starless night never to return. It may have been that he fell asleep and a sudden blast of wind made his vessel turn. Or he may have drunk too much wine on the eve of the Shabbat. Over the years, many conjectures were brought up about his fate, and some claimed Nissim Ezekiel had migrated to England, while others held he had been seen at a temple of Kali down south in the Subcontinent. Yet others thought he had married a Dravidian prostitute and was devotedly sharing with her his meagre earnings. The community which saw his birth grew larger; winds of wealth raised families and enlarged households. Gardens became greener and lusher. So much so that old friends stopped visiting each other, and women did not gather to cook anymore.

One morning of Hanukah, the Feast of Lights, Ephraim Baghdadi arrived at Konkan and asked about Nissim Ezekiel, whom he had taught a little and from whom he had learned much. It struck him as strange that he had vanished without leaving a trace, although looking well upon it, such a fate had also befallen Moses, whose burial place, near Mount Nebo, was still unknown. There was also nothing further known about the chariot of the Prophet Elias. Furthermore, was it not common in India, that upon reaching the age of wrinkles people would leave everything behind to sail upstream on the Ganges?

"I remember what he used to say," recalled a woman who had met the visitor from Bombay, "as he faced the moon: 'May our building help us unite and not be separated.'"

Ephraim Baghdadi smiled: those were his own words, varnished over by the years, but still recognisable.

"And so it is," he sighed, squinting in order to better evoke his friend. "Those who, on the wake of their death, leave objects and property promote rivalry, dissension and fences, but those who leave words are sowing passage and alliances—bread made with syllables for the mouths of the future."

It is often said that the moon, lebanah לבנה, *has the same root as the word* bniyah בניה, *building. Thus, what the sun projects is articulated by the moon; what the greater star designs is materialised by the gentle mistress of the night. But if it happens that the thickness of a building obstructs the osmotic principle of dialogue, then walls and fences separate mouths from the fluent purpose of their words. And then, instead of wise men, a community is left solely with owners.*

Yoshka the Hunchback, Thief of Twitters

There lived in the forests of Moldavia a hunchback butcher everybody called Yoshka the thief of twitters, because his major amusement was going in the spring to the most obscure areas of the woods, setting a decoy trap, thus catching some jay or bunting, which he would tease into singing to somehow unravel their simple melodies, and finally let them go back into the good air of God. Malicious tongues surmised that he rubbed the wild birds against his hunch in order to have their music straighten what his mother's weep, upon seeing him so frail, had contributed to bend. Good tongues, instead, held that Yoshka ought to know the location of the Earthly Paradise, called in the *Zohar*, or *Book of Splendour*, nothing less than *The Bird's Nest*. Otherwise, they said, it was impossible to explain his ability.

Having learnt about Yoshka, the thief of twitters, Rabbi Amos ben Eliezer of Turda asked to meet him during one of his trips across the region.

"He is much too humble a man, Master," they told him.

"Not very cleanly," they explained.

"Of very few words," they clarified.

But as the master insisted, they went for Yoshka the hunchback, whom they found, now past the joys of Easter, cleaning his cages and gathering crusts and crumbs of bread.

"I want to see how you work, Yoshka, what you do in the woods," Rabbi Amos said to him respectfully, getting only a dubious nod as a reply from the hunchback, who was in the habit of going alone on his excursions. "I mean it: our Mishnah tells us we must learn everything from everyone, and that there is no knowledge, however useless it may seem, which is not a form of happiness," he told him in order to win him over.

The following day they prayed after washing their hands, then drank a strong tea and set off, the Rabbi and the hunchback alone together. The master noticed with wonder that Yoshka would tweet under the tall fir trees, by the rocking shadow of the birches, and that upon his call countless birds of different colours would come, which fluttered around his hunch as they eagerly awaited his crumbs. The heart of the master beat faster when he remembered a quotation from the *Zohar* that goes: "The voice of the turtle-dove was the voice of God heard for the first time upon earth after the creation of man...," exactly when one of them was alighting! Afterwards, barely recovered from the surprising synchronicity, he remembered Solomon's loquacious hoopoe, the seer goldfinch of Sultan Alkabul, and the dwarf peacock of the Celebes, of which they said it would utter your name if you managed to hold its gaze long enough. But none of these winged creatures inhabited these regions.

Yoshka then set his first trap, and he waited with half-closed eyes. When a finch finally arrived and he captured it, he whistled something, then pricked up his ears to listen to its fearful call and smiled, looking at his companion to tell him:

"There are three kinds of twitters, and this bird sings the last one."

"What are they?" Rabbi Amos of Turda wanted to know.

"The first one says: the sky has limits, but I cross them. The second one: the sky has no limits, and there where I sing is the centre of the world. And finally, the third one goes: the sky is my third wing, sustaining me beyond weariness and oblivion."

"Where have you learnt all these things? I find it hard to believe from the sole eloquence of the twitters," avowed the rabbi.

"Do you perchance ignore," answered the hunchback, "that for whoever believes in them, birds form part of his own self, and that the reverse of the self is an uninterrupted song owing them more than one chirp?"

The verb to believe is in Hebrew he'amin האמין, *and even though it is unlikely that a simpleton such as the hunchback would be coining puns, the Talmud says that ever since the destruction of the Second Temple, wisdom speaks through the mouth of children and fools. The verb mentioned contains the words I,* ani אני, *and they,* hem הם, *which shows that the question asked by the rabbi was well answered by Yoshka the butcher. Furthermore, when a question is answered with another question, surely the answer is in the possession of whoever asked in the first place.*

Death and the Thistle

Rabbi Anatoli Lifshitz of Riga used to say:

"Well looked upon, death has two thirds of perfection. Otherwise, how could our deceased, once past the panting irregularity of agony, exhibit such calm, relaxed faces?"

The master and his disciples were walking through the Russian steppes on a summer afternoon shortly after the rain. The grass and the herbage had grown tall. Birds were busy enjoying their feast of insects. That year the emperor had succeeded in restraining his Cossacks, and the Jews could walk more peacefully through the muddy streets of their bleak villages.

"On the last summer I went to meet our master, Rabbi Alexander Ismael Midot of Sarajevo," continued Anatoli Lifshitz of Riga as he plucked a violet thistle from the roadside without fear of its thorns. "Our beloved master, an expert in brews and proverbs, cut then, just as I did now, a thistle, and explained to me the following: 'The Torah likens Israel to the rose among the thorns, but it seems to me that for a very long time our life has been more like the thistle, rugged and prickly at the stalk, and only tender and perfumed when it looks upwards, opening its composite flower. Day after day we are little more than beasts of burden, and we take our own braying for wisdom, when most of the time we are but letting out hoarse and disconnected sounds. However, it is not uncommon that at the moment of dying, like the thistle, with the *Shema* in our mouths, our minds open almost entirely to the violet of the Spirit, exhibiting the ineffable smile of the angels.'"

The disciples knew that the presumptive Alexander Ismael Midot of Sarajevo was a fiction of Rabbi Anatoli, as were

THE LIVING PALM TREE

Rabbi Isaiah of Tarko-Sale and Rabbi Uri of Orsk, hypostases or mouthpieces for the master himself to say through others' tongues what came in abundance from his own. But even so they believed him, for with the course of centuries, someone somewhere might indeed have that name, and he could then come to easily and ingenuously quote the very words Rabbi Anatoli used now to speak to them. Sons of Adam after all, we are descendants from the same father. On what grounds should we privilege one generation over another, a real mouth before an imaginary one?

> *The Hebrew words death,* mavet מות, *and thistle,* qimosh קמוש, *have the same numerical value of 446. As for death having some measure of perfection, this is ascertained by the fact that two of its key letters, when read together, form the word* tam תם, *perfect, innocent, whole.*

The Times of the Cherry Tree

From all the phrases, sentences, teachings and parables in the Bible, Rabbi Ezekiel of Radom, son to the famous scribe Itzi of Radom, preferred the one from *Ecclesiastes* 3:11 which says: "He hath made every thing beautiful in its time: also He hath set eternity in their hearts." And every time he had a chance, he would explain again the reason for this choice, as if he still found hard to acknowledge the illumination produced by his understanding of it, and as if he wished, by evoking it, to make it more and more profound.

"It took place under a cherry tree," he used to explain, "near the beginning of June. The tree was so full with fruits, and they were so shiny that they resembled big drops of blood an instant before their coagulation. I was witnessing the birds' quarrels, the tickling of the leaves, the creeping of the first butterfly grubs, when suddenly, lo and behold, I caught the delay of a flower which in a nook of shade had missed the sun's signal for it to close down. Thus, I told myself, this cherry tree gathers in itself every time: the one of youth and the one of ripening, the dead phases of its bark, the hard days of its wounds, the sweet hours of its fruits, and the bitter ones of its branches broken through excessive weight. I was rapt in that perfect contemplation when I felt in my chest, amplified by the grace of the instant, the soft beat of the human cherry, my own heart—the rhythm of its alternating flow under my skin."

Upon reaching this point in his narrative, no matter where he was, Rabbi Ezekiel of Radom would take his right hand to his thorax; he would sigh, half-closing his eyes, and then he would quote in Hebrew: *ha-olam natan be-libam* העלם נתן בלבם,

"He hath set eternity in their hearts," thus conclusively giving as understood, for whoever would be listening, one of the most enigmatic verses of the Scriptures.

Afterwards, more relaxed, he would add:

"When, grateful for that vision, I embraced the cherry tree, I realised in an instant that by referring myself to my own intimacy I was satisfying my spiritual longing; I was pushing myself towards the dark estuary of my blood, where eternity is a cordial fact which heartbeats keep in synchronicity with time. Out there, on the cherry tree, all its ages were present in their full embodiment. Inside here," Rabbi Ezekiel of Radom said, rubbing his breastbone, "inside here all our blood cells keep at play with the universe.

The phrase "in their hearts", be-libam בלבם *(74), is numerically equivalent to* lomed *or* lamad למד*, to learn, to study, to be taught. It is for this reason that they say, within the circles of students of Kabbalah, that knowledge is centrifugal and wisdom centripetal. This on condition that we go away, if we ever really do so, only to better return to ourselves.*

The Best Way

Every time his work as a professional circumciser made him take the road, Rabbi Obadiah Raphael of Marrakesh would read Psalm 27:11: "Teach me your way, O God," not because he felt unsure about the righteousness of his steps, or his knowledge of the towns and villages he went through, where he occasionally had to spend the night, or because haste would force him to take faster ways through shorter paths. No, he read it because he needed to have the certainty that he walked at every moment under the light of the Most High, in pain as in grace, in temporary abandonment as in intimate satisfaction.

"The way to men is made up of steps," he used to say, "but the way from and towards the Creator is made up of deeds. Our steps must have the firm consolation of a supporting foothold; they owe the heels their leverage and the toes their continuity, but our deeds are not measured the instant we perform them, nor are they judged the instant they become manifest, and they are only grounded on a fickle soul which changes emotions as the clouds change their form and course."

"It seems," his study companion Rabbi Gershom Azuly commented one day, "from what the psalm lets us guess, as if the Creator had only one way, one single path. Otherwise, the sentence should offer us a plural form, shouldn't it?"

"Mother-of-pearl is one, but its reflections are many," replied Rabbi Obadiah Raphael. "We know that the way to Him is the good one when before our eyes, and due to our own deeds, the blissful iris of other's smile shines out. If the way is good, a very good one, the foot feels winged. And if our relations to others are just, then it is not necessary to explain ourselves, to question

THE LIVING PALM TREE

why we act as we do. The economy of gestures fosters richness of thought, and everything—everything around us—weighs a little less."

"May it be so," smiled Rabbi Gershom Azuly.

"Take this," replied his friend, offering him a luminous piece of mother-of-pearl, "a sea compass to walk the earth, a shell to admire here and now."

The sentence from the psalm quoted reads in Hebrew: horeni adonai darkekha הוריני יהוה דרכך, *but we can also read "your way",* darkekha דרכך, *as a combination of two other words,* dar דר, *mother-of-pearl, and* kakh ךכ, *thus, in such a way. The* Book of Brightness, *or* Bahir, *of the twelfth century, dwells at length upon this mysterious stone or substance of organic origin called* dar: *"The Holy One, Blessed be He, took a thousandth part from the power of that light, and He created with it a precious substance* (dar) *in which He included all commandments."*

On the Reverse of the Word Sleep

A man called Manasseh came to visit Rabbi Oded Malachi of Tangiers for him to help solve a problem.

"They say that the words of our Torah are, amongst other things," he confided, "doors of syllables opening onto the world of serenity. As I have trouble sleeping, I have thought that if I managed to open the door of the word sleep, occurring in Jeremiah 31:26, where it says: 'Upon this I awaked, and beheld; and my sleep was sweet unto me,' then perhaps I could truly rest, for I am sure that on the other side I shall find some formula that promotes repose, or at least some sort of consolation. Do you know how the doors of words are opened?"

Rabbi Oded stroke his beard. This man was asking a breathtaking question: he had never heard it said that the words of the teaching were doors leading to the world of serenity. They would certainly grant beauty, encouragement, inspiration, and they would sharpen your understanding, but as for serenity...

"Have you tried drinking a lime tree infusion?" he attempted as an answer. "It is sometimes our nerves that will not let us sleep well."

Respectfully, the man returned home with the rabbi's advice, forgetting for a while about the doors of words, but Oded Malachi opened his Tanakh looking for the verse in question, and he fell asleep as he meditated on its letters and numbers.

Thus it was, he told his friends afterwards, that the doors of Jeremiah's passage opened for him, and he found himself walking over a sea of clouds whose waves were future dreams, and whose fading outlines resembled endless shores. Later, when he woke up, he understood that serenity is a weightless gift, a soft atmospheric lapse without any support or grasp, and that this same feeling was bestowed by the Torah. The following day he made his way to the dwelling of the insomniac to whom he had recommended an infusion, meaning to apologise.

"Forgive me," he said to him, "I know how the words are opened, and I did not tell you."

"I understood you perfectly," the man replied. "The hot water opened the dry lime leaves, and I drank the entire cup and procured a sleep so perfect that I did not need to bother the prophet."

"Well done," sighed Oded Malachi. "The useful is not always straightforward. On the other side of words there are other words that refer us to this side."

"Thank you," the man managed to say, "thank you anyway for this unexpected visit."

What makes one man sleep will awaken another, what dulls one, amazes another. The lime tree is called in Hebrew tirzah תרזה, *and it holds within a secret splendour, or* zohar זהר, *for whoever is able to see it.*

The Son of the Sea of Air

In his youth, when he worked as a chemistry lecturer in Berlin around the time of the beginning of the century, Rabbi Yoshuah Erlich, who was then not yet a rabbi, heard a Polish Jew saying that the Baal Shem Tob, the Master of the Good Name, founder of the Hasidic movement, used to go to meditate in the forest and become rapt with the green transparency of the leaves, through whose nerves he had realised that besides being a son of his family, he was also a scion of the air surrounding the trees.

"I am a son of the sea of air," the Baal Shem Tob used to proclaim. "Its waves support me, and my lungs teach my blood how to swim in the foam of the breeze."

"We thought you had been born in the mountains, Master," his friends and disciples would tell him.

"As if there was no air in them," smiled the Baal Shem. "It happens that out of laziness we number our birthdays based on what is visible, without ever considering the days, minutes and seconds of our invisible and silent breathing; but it is there where neither linear time nor genealogy count, because from the skin inwards we owe everything, or almost everything, to our parents and ancestors, but from the skin outwards, from the very tip of our nose, we owe everything to the Living Creator, who is right now hovering in the sea of air, breath after breath.

Twenty years after hearing this story, and in the manner of St Paul falling from his horse, Yoshuah Erlich of Berlin fell from a ladder in his laboratory, crashing against a window and luckily breaking only the glass thereof. Now, the March breeze wafting through and entering his nostrils was so laden with early spring perfume as with spiritual aroma. And thus ever since, the chemist changed his test tubes for Kabbalah texts; he transmuted sulphur, alcohol and vanity to silence and meditation, and one day, when he had already become Rabbi Yoshua Erlich of Berlin, he left aside the research of ozone, whose blue colour he had helped discover, and whose purity he was certain of, and he repeated to himself that he was also, at last, a son of the sea of air—a traveller of boundless space.

There where Psalm 2:7 reads ha-yom הים, *today, in the sentence "My Son; this day have I begotten thee,"* בני אתה אני הים ילדתיך, *many scholars read* ha-yam הים, *the sea. Now, as the letter* hei ה *stands for the breath, the soul, both Baal Shem, perhaps unknowingly, and Rabbi Yoshuah Erlich of Berlin, knowing the value of oxygen in its relation to the Spirit, declare themselves to be sons of that which goes beyond and comes nearer than our biological ancestors.*

Panting or Inspiring

Rabbi Mikhail Volodin of Sarajevo, a surveyor, translator and miniaturist, used to ramble around the city markets and antique shops looking for brass objects such as inkwells, magnifying glass stands or rasps, a search which made him acquainted with junk dealers, gypsies and all sorts of pilferers. When he travelled to Jerusalem in the company of his disciple Rabbi Amiram Obadieh of Tirana, they were both seasick aboard their ship, which made the master recall the following:

"Once, in a market in Edessa, where I got a beautiful eighteenth century English spyglass—probably stolen from an embassy—a gypsy heard me sighing, upon which he asked me: 'What kind of man are you? Are you of those who pant, or are you of those who inspire and are inspired?' Looking at him with bewilderment, I replied with another question: 'What do you mean?' 'Those who pant, and go through their lives sighing as if they had just run a hundred metres sprint,' he told me, 'are usually horses of others, donkeys of many, and mules of themselves.' 'What about those who inspire and are inspired?' I queried. 'Ah,' said the gypsy, who was one-eyed, and dusky like a blackbird, 'there are very few of those. They are the ones who, when facing any situation, either pleasant or unpleasant, thrust their chest out, drawing breath and getting ready in case there is something else to live, as nothing seems too much to them. Their character is like a prow, and they break through reality as boats break the waves, making the foam crackle.'"

Rabbi Amiram Obadieh of Tirana, who had barely recovered from his latest bout of sickness, managed to comment:

"A hidden sage, it seems to me. Or in any case a good observer."

THE LIVING PALM TREE

"He knew a little Yiddish, and I knew some Rumanian," Mikhail Volodin of Sarajevo continued, "so we went to share a coffee in order to deepen our dialogue. Once he saw I was interested in his ideas he carried on:

"'He who sighs and pants, if you watch him closely, wants to quickly finish whatever he is doing; he would throw in the towel at any minute, which he feels is wet due to his prenatal fatigue. But he who inspires and is inspired would like everything to come to him in a double share, even calamities, in order to try himself and prove to himself not only that the air is still good, but even more, that there is plenty for everyone.'"

The ship on which master and disciple were travelling came into port in the most complete stillness, since it was September, and the sea was as smooth and shiny as it was calm. They strolled through Haifa for a while as they stretched their legs; Rabbi Mikhail Volodin of Sarajevo uttering a blessing to the Creator for the fig he had just bought and was about to eat, and Amiram Obadieh of Tirana trying—without his companion noticing—to change his usual desolate sighs for inspirations.

Eliezer Ben Yehudah Surrounded by Words

They say, but it is difficult to know with any certainty, that whenever Eliezer Ben Yehudah, the re-creator of modern Hebrew, who lived in Jerusalem surrounded by dictionaries of Coptic, Greek, Aramaic, Latin, German, and all sorts of Biblical lexicons, that whenever he was looking for a word in the Torah, intending to graft it onto another in order to obtain a third one fitting what he needed to name, that the angel of language, Safael, who assisted him unawares, would turn like a fast whirlwind on his rainbow wings, then ascend up to the divine Throne and ask the Creator about the legal validity of the whole procedure. How is it possible, some would question on seeing his efforts, to transform a sacred language into a profane instrument without falling prey to the fevers of prophecy or without falling into the archaic dilemma of the judges or the praising intoxication of the psalmist? This was an irresolvable mystery. His work, indeed, implied enormous risks, and required a wise serenity. On the one hand, there were those who supported the linguist, those who encouraged him to keep finding adjectives, striking the right tones, renewing functions, lightening nouns; and on the other hand there were his detractors, old Talmudists shipwrecked in a sea of prayers, with no help other than a highborn order which was, by definition, safe; rabbis angered at modernity, poetry, and at the sacred being available to children and women—at once wise men of the trivial and keepers of the ashes of the wonderful.

Eliezer Ben Yehudah was a man of small build, with highly polished spectacles and attentive eyes. Combining the passion of a stamp collector with the rigour of a chemist, he would take apart triliteral roots and play with prefixes and suffixes, passive and active voices, out of use verbs and new inventions, trying to kindle in his child what he found to be dormant in the millenary archives of his people. One afternoon Rabbi Eliahu Sorek of Vilna paid him a visit. He was one of the few religious personalities who respected him and tolerated this apparently profane endeavour of the obsessed grammarian. He was younger than Eliezer, but he looked older, for his beard reached down almost to his belly. His green eyes had the meekness of a river pool, but his knuckles, those of a binder of holy books, were as strong and decisive as vine shoots.

"Tell me, Eliezer," he asked Ben Yehudah, "amongst all the words found, reconstructed, polished and restored to circulation in daily speech, amongst all the terms of our holy language, which is the one that has afforded you the most happiness?"

The linguist did not reply immediately. He went to his library and came back with a copy of an engraving attributed to Schwann, the author of cell theory. It was an intricate maze of concentric circles, dots, nuclei and alveoli.

"Listen to these words," he said: "The elementary parts of tissues are formed by cells according to similar modalities, although diversified, so that you could say there exists a universal development principle for the essential parts of organisms, and that this principle is the formation of cells."

Silence grew thick in the studio sheltering the two men, the religious one and the layman.

"The Hebrew word you ask me about, my dear friend," Ben Yehudah then continued, "the word for whose preservation and restoration I would give my life if needed, is our *et* את, composed by the first and the last letters of our alphabet, which is also, when inversed, *ta* תא, the cell."

Rabbi Eliahu Sorek of Vilna could still not understand, and he intervened:

"*Et* for us means *Or Torah* אור תורה, the Light of the Teaching, but it is also *Eben Tabon* אבן תבון, the Stone of Discernment."

"Unknowingly," the linguist carried on, "and while he conducted his biological research, Schwann was rediscovering the mysticism of the Kabbalah, which affirms that all words, adverbs, gerunds and prepositions, and indeed all language, is built upon that basic unit, *et* or *ta*, and as likely to become our gaol as our freedom."

"Our gaol? Why our gaol?"

"It is so: a cell can as easily be a living cell as a prison cell. Furthermore, the Romans saw in *cella* also a granary, the place where you keep your food. This is why, if a word does not feed you, if language is a prison cell for you instead of a living cell, if it oppresses you and distresses you and locks you within its repetitive solemnity, it will be something dead for you. But if it is something living and throbbing, if it expands and blooms, engulfing a new sky and a new earth, then it will enliven you, exalt you, and it will transform you so that you can at last say, as Schwann himself: 'The cause of nutrition and growth lies not in the totality of an organism, but in its elementary parts: the cells.' Likewise, our survival is also in that word, that particle of light by which we have been nourished for more than three thousand years."

"I understand now," said Rabbi Eliahu Sorek with a half-smile.

"The word for which I live and die, for which I am reborn and I work, for which I smile and weep is *et*, the beginning and end of our language, its feminine *you* protecting us and holding us."

That the same root, formed by the letters aleph *and* tau, *is used to indicate the verbal accusative as well as to name the cell, the living cell, and that this very root is at the same time the feminine pronoun* at, *you, all this is too much to be understood at once, since the semantic here becomes ontological. On another front, based on Revelation 1:8, where mention is made of the letters* alpha *and* omega *(ΑΩ), early Christianity would make of this Hebrew polysemy* the principle upon which is established the Mystical Body of the believers united by the Holy Ghost. *Only that, while hidden in Greek, the principle in question becomes evident when we understand that the Hebrew digraph* ta את *is the basic unit of Biblical language as a whole, its primordial cell.*

Black Fire, White Fire

About to fall under the cruel grasp of the Roman legions at Qumran, Rabbi Barak Gilgul took his young disciple Yehiel to the ritual bath. This happened before dawn. The most nimble of the Essenes were high up in the caves, putting away their remaining sacred texts to keep them from falling into the hands of the invaders. Further south the smoke of fire and destruction was rising in sad and slender eddies.

"There is a passage in Daniel 11:35 which warns us," observed Rabbi Barak with a trembling voice, " 'Some of the wise shall fall, to try them, and to purge and to make them white, to the time of the end: for it shall yet be for the time appointed.' "

Both of them, master and disciple, plunged in the cold water which had a taste of bitter herbs. At that very moment, not far from them, those who defended Masada were taking each other's lives, but neither the old master nor the young scribe knew or would ever know about it.

"I invest you," began Rabbi Barak once he had dried himself, "with the white tunic of our community, so that you come to be a true son of the heart, an altar of praise whose freedom is unbribable and from whose music we live."

Roman legionaries had set fire to the fortress gates, and after their long siege they were ready to ruthlessly storm in. Judea would be finally vanquished in its most harsh desert quarters, at the farthest dependencies of Herod's summer palace. Shortly afterwards they would go for the solitaries, those magicians and doctors of the soul who lived on the shores of Sea of Salt.

"I receive it with honour," replied Yehiel, "and I shall pass with happiness from difference to likeness, from solitude to communion, from the mirror to the light."

"Our sages," sighed the old master wearily, "held that the Torah was conferred on Mount Sinai with two kinds of fire, black and white. Due to the darkness of its letters, to the irregularity of its profile, the world is created in a series of opposites, from contrary to contrary; but due to the peaceful whiteness which groups them from above and below, the universe is re-created in light, from circle into circle, from wave into wave. Thus it is, and thus it will be. In the likeness of coal, with souls extinguished, Romans pursue a fate of mere ashes and iron, while our task—like the glow of a dying flame—has been to sow with solar hymns the ways of the Eternal One. This is why no peace is possible between us. No physician can cure omnipotence in an ailing one, nor, far from home, does the soldier tread the ground compassionately. They work for discord and taxes; we to further concord and grace. They think they are oppressing a small people, and they do but prepare to reveal its greatness to the world. Be prepared then, Yehiel, to wear with this tunic the sign of those who return clarity for clarity."

The silence inside the fortress of Masada was complete. Beyond the blood-stained rocks, the legionaries caught sight of the blue woollen strands of a doll in the hands of a girl who had died with wide open eyes. In Qumran, however, within the ascetic halls of the Essenes, there were no colours other than the black and the white—and eyes to see them unfold their dance upon the land of the ancestors.

The sect of the Essenes, who, between the 2nd century BC and the 1st century AD, were devoted to medicine, meditation, and to the copying and preservation of traditional Hebrew sacred texts, used to initiate their members by investing them with a white linen tunic. On its rim were knotted the thirty-two paths of wisdom of the Kabbalah, as in the tallit, or praying mantle, still worn today by the Jews. Since the word for white is in the language of the Bible laban לבן, containing both the son, ben בן, and the heart, leb לב, every initiate had to assume that his own body was all the family he had. They had to see in each of their organs a sibling, in every sigh a dead self, and in every breath a subtle rebirth from the breath of the Only One. The Essenes also held that under this colour was hidden, transliterated yet whole, the lute, or nebel נבל, *of the vertebrae, able to change noise into melody, and oblivion into memory.*

Ecstasy under the Vault of Shade

According to the different times of the year, the Ancient of Days used to take his disciple Lo-Yadua out on a walk through the different quarters of Jerusalem. In winter, he preferred the distant hillocks, the very limits of the city, where there were the stones of a colour reminiscent of tea with milk, keeping a strong grasp on some perfumed shrubs. In spring, they would travel to the Judaean desert, to watch the flowering lilies and listen to the Beduins' melancholy music. But it was the hot summers that the master really enjoyed, and he would encourage others to enjoy his walks through Rehavia, among streets whose names evoke Ibn Ezra or Alharizi, mediaeval Hebrew poets, kindred souls long gone, yet still alive in the resounding measure of their verses.

"Observe this vault of vegetal coolness," he said one morning to Lo-Yadua. "May is a feast of branches and an explosion of roses for hearts thirsting after beauty. Every time I walk down this way, I am overcome by such a feeling of gratitude, that I touch every tree, every bench, every myrtle and every stone with devotion, as if they had just been newly created."

"A minimal space for an enormous feeling," commented Lo-Yadua, the Unknown.

"I would rather say," the old man commented, "that this is one centre of the world."

"You say one, as if there were many. Are there really so many?"

"A dozen, perhaps two, or even less."

"And how would you define them? How would you explain what a centre of the world is?"

"In the likeness of what our sages have always done, with a pun, which is at the same time a subtle swaying of the spirit within the orb of their feelings."

"I am all ears, Master," smiled Lo-Yadua.

"If, instead of reading *merkaz* מרכז, centre, you read *raz mimkha* רז ממך, your secret, written with the same letters, then after their positions have been altered, you will discover that arriving at the centre of the world means discovering your own mystery, the throbbing ecstasy beneath your awestruck veins. We spend our life travelling, coming and going, disheartened and restless, to and fro, and only rarely do we have the feeling that we have arrived somewhere. But when our being and our location do coincide, then Being Itself wraps with Its whirl of light the helicoid of Its shadows, and it seems to us we are being held without hands in the miracle of perplexity—until what must take place does so: the last of your sighs appears, between your sternum and your navel, to be the first one of them all, for breathing is a treasure open through your nostrils. Doubtlessly, under this shady vault," he added, pointing towards the tall and lush pines, "the will abdicates for perception to be reborn; intention falls, for spontaneity to rise."

Then, after a few silent seconds, he remarked:

"Listen—a nightingale is singing, yesterday's water still dripping from its beak."

Jerusalem, like Mecca or Cuzco, is one of those centres of the world where our species has treasured awakenings and enlightenments, psychic transmutations and endless joys. Now, the Ancient in our story sustains that merkaz מרכז, *centre, can be unfolded as raz mimkha* רז ממך, *your secret, or your mystery, whence he who reaches his own centre reveals to himself his own enigma. That is the place where he belongs completely to himself, and where he can therefore surrender himself completely.*

Sulphur and Musk

On board the aeroplane which took him from Addis Ababa to Israel during Operation Moses, Rabbi Obed Ge'ezi, his eyes blinded by cataracts, carried with him a piece of sulphur and a piece of musk, as a memento of his days as a poor Felasha, when he outweighed his meagre earnings as a goldsmith with the trade in what was then known as fragrance stones, mother substances for the production of remedies and essences. The musk came from Karachi, but it had been earlier in the hands of a Muslim tradesman from the Kandahar region. The sulphur piece, in turn, had been bought at the Aden market.

"Why are you taking these hand-worn stones to Israel, Father?" asked his son, Abiach Ge'ezi.

"In my youth I got lost in the desert, with scarcely any water and under a head-splitting sun. I was on my way, or was supposed to be going, from Sana' to Khaybar, but my mules died, my load was stolen from me, and I could only hide in my clothes this piece of sulphur and this remnant of musk, tokens of Hell and Paradise, between which we always stand. I think it was them—these stones—that saved my life."

"You had never told me, Father," said Abiach Ge'ezi, looking with wonder at the sinuous Red Sea shoreline. It was the first time in his thirty years that he had travelled by aeroplane.

" 'The universe is held together by its secrets,' so say our sages," observed Rabbi Obed Ge'ezi. "And now that we return home after so many centuries," he added, "I can be frank with you: just as Hell has to do with our bottom, even so, Paradise depends on our mouth. It is for this reason that the smell down there is often of death and sulphur, while up here, between our lips, scanty and yet present, the good word springs up perfumed for our own benefit and that of others."

Amazed, Abiach Ge'ezi looked at his father as if he were looking at another person—someone distraught by this flight over the burning Arabian desert, the same Happy Arabia, *Arabia Felix*, did he but know it, whence mythical myrrh and incense sprang from, the very same *terra speciorum* of ancient times.

"Hell is the place of what is undone, and Paradise the place of what is done," Rabbi Obed Ge'ezi went on, opening wide his veiled eyes. "Like the musk deer from which this stone comes, we tend towards Paradise when all our messages are love calls, and we shall not move away from Hell unless our deeds become edible fruits, living and fragrant works—healthy waters for the thirst of many."

"But then," his son sighed with a certain dismay, "we will always be in the middle, between Paradise and Hell, hanging from our mouths above and depending on our bottoms from below."

"You are wrong," his father smiled. "We are always, as we are now, in flight, in movement, oscillating, and this is what human grace consists of—the right swing. If you go too low, the stench of sulphur fills you with disdain, and once and again you are expelled from the body of life; but if you go instead too high, the musky smell of your pride loses you, the fragrance of your vanity stuns you, and then you are estranged from those who need you. You must swing like your own heart, and there will not be a place you cannot reach, no compassion you cannot feel, no joy which is barred to you. Only when the extremities are known is the wisdom of the centre attained."

In 1984, during what is known as Operation Moses, 15,000 Felashas, Jews from a hunger- and poverty-stricken Ethiopia, travelled undercover to Israel in one of the most amazing airlifts of modern history, especially since the travellers were not only moving through space, but also from the Middle Ages to the 20th century in a matter of hours. To oscillate or to swing is in Hebrew hitnoded התנדד, *whose most obvious component is nod* נד, *to err, to wander; but since the remaining letters of the word form, in turn, the expression ha-dat* הדת, *the reli-*

gion, it is likely that its true sense is in teaching us to harmoniously swing between the Hell of expulsions and the Paradise of integrations.

The Root of the Past and the Cup of the Future

"Look at that tree," said Rabbi Ephraim of Baghdad to his disciple Yochanan, pointing towards an orange tree growing in the yard of their study house. "Its roots sink in the past, while the leaves of its branches prepare their own future."

The moment had a taste of fresh water, mint and lemon. They were in the summer of big moons, in the season of golden peaches, and the swifts shrieked joyfully above them, for the air was full with tiny insects.

"Slow and dark, the past in us is also feeding on humus and death," Ephraim of Baghdad went on. "It lives on corpses and fermentations, but also on fixities and constancies, whence he who does not love his past is as one who despised his ancestors and who ignored the secret of the earth."

"What secret, Master?" Yochanan wanted to know.

Twilight was falling, and imperceptibly for the two men, the branches of the orange tree leant down a little towards the ground.

"It is the earth, mistress of the dust and keeper of the seed, it is she who teaches us that repose is joy, and that support is continuity. Its secret lies in its having a measure for everything," the old rabbi observed, "whereas heaven, like our future, has no ground and no limits; it thrives on the perpetual flight of its light and the turning of its stars. This is why we are not free from the past, but we are free from the morrow. A tomorrow which is formed by these green leaves you see, swaying in the late afternoon hours. Whoever thinks his future is meaningless, knows nothing about the green alternation guiding the branches, and he ignores the secret of heaven."

"What secret, master?" Yochanan asked again.

"It is heaven, preparing the waters yet to come, out of those which have been, it is He Who wants us brought near Him through the mediation of the wind generated by the two waters. Its secret is called infinite, but its revelation, in its entirety, will fit in your mouth's palate, and in your pupils' glow."

"I can see you like to raise enigmas, Rabbi Ephraim," said the disciple.

"What I like is to thread conjectures with sighs, and then to weave wonderments. This tree, the orange tree, being a friend of time, why would it not be ours too?"

In the Hebrew word adamah אדמה, *earth, we find the root* midah, מדה, *measure, as also within heaven,* shamaym שמים, *we find* maym מים, *the plural waters. Because it is the tendency of the leaf to grow upwards, the future is said to be ascensional, and given that the root is ever so constantly sticking fast to the ground, it is believed that respecting the past hidden under its surface will give us both persistence and stability.*

Light for the Nations

"We read in *Isaiah* 49:6," said Rabbi Alexis Suares of Alexandria to his disciples, as they journeyed through the desert near Lake Mareotis, "that we shall be given as a light for the nations, *le'or goyim* לאור גיים, a task as sublime as oppressive."

"I can understand that it is sublime, Master," one of his disciples observed, "but oppressive, why should it be oppressive?"

"Light has always annoyed those who sleep," the master confided, "and this is why it is the awakened ones who are always grateful for clarity upon clarity. Indeed, observe that the passage quoted speaks of nations without specifying how many or which ones, and that light, when it manifests, does nothing but define, show, uncover, encompass and separate. Hence it is, or it will be, oppressive to have to shed light on those who do not wish to leave confusion and ambiguity, those who prefer to hide within the crowd. One ray of light too many, and in exchange for our light we may receive hatred, rejection and scorn."

It was the second sunrise of spring, and patches in the desert were glimmering everywhere after the rain, hundreds of birds were flying over, and the master made ready to show his disciples a copy of the Cairo Genizah texts, ancient synagogue documents discovered decades earlier and now in the possession of some Western museum. Three years before this outing which brought together master and disciples, the Gnostic texts of Nag Hammadi had been found at Jabal al-Tarif, a mountain in which there were more than one hundred and fifty caves, a finding that had made the Christian world as excited as it was upset.

"What can we do, then?" asked another of the walkers. "Should we silence our discoveries, mask our illuminations, restrain our flickering?"

"Oh, no," the master smiled, "nothing of the sort. We must remember, remember, and not forget at any moment that we are in the world to highlight the freedom of its hues, and that the light revealing them, an infinite principle within man, asks of him, who is finite, to be evoked every time he strives to rediscover his origin."

Master Alexis Suares is hinting at a gematria, or subtle numerical correspondence, by which we ascertain that to illumine or give light, le'or לאור *(237), is like remembering,* yizkor זכר, *whence that, almost platonically, light and memory are identical. Furthermore, as we evoke the symbolic value of the three letters composing the word* or אור, *light, we can see that* alef *refers to infinity within man, who is represented by the letter* vav ו, *contained in turn, in its manifestation, within the principle set by the letter* reish ר.

The Master and the Essence

Every time Rabbi Yo'ab Zofar of Yemen was called "Master" by one of his pupils, he used to reply:

"We are all masters, the cobbler and the blacksmith, the singing bird and the sewing dressmaker, the lizard finding its way between two rocks and the ray of light wounding the clouds. What is difficult is to be a disciple; what is strenuous is to remain a student until the last day of our lives.

"What is then, in your opinion," they enquired, "the difference between a master and a disciple? Or better still: why is it easier to teach than to learn, when in reality both actions are inseparable, and when logic tells us that we first learn, then we transmit what we have learnt?"

"To be wise is essential," Rabbi Yo'ab Zofar would reply, "it is in the nature of things, since *rabi* רבי, master, and *bori* ברי, essence, have the same letters. We are born knowing, but we forget as we grow older, we lose our inquisitiveness and we acquire pride; our innocence dwindles, while our self-regard, sadly, increases. You see, how many of us dedicate ourselves, with happiness and devotion, to learning and to making use of what we have already learnt? How many are there who reclaim their very own treasures and are ready to be lifelong students, preserving the purity of children as well as their adventurous fearlessness? It seems to me that the trap into which masters fall is in a 'sitting' thought: the vanity of believing there is a fixed fulcrum; whereas students are spared this thanks to the restlessness of their feet and the thirst of their mouths which take them to and fro among the sources of the world."

"But you are yourself sitting right now," his younger students laughed.

"It is true," the master laughed back, rising and thus revealing his worn-out seat, "but my chair has no seat. In this way I keep my bottom in the void, to make my head get used to the same in heaven."

The Hebrew words rabi רבי, *master, and* bori ברי, *essential, natural, evident, indeed make use of the same letters in their spelling, whereas disciple,* talmid תלמיד, *is formed by the words* yeled ילד, *child, and* tamid תמיד, *which means always. Moreover, we can see that professors' chairs are somewhat in opposition to the philosophical knowledge of the* Peripatetics, *or those who learn while walking.*

The Spiral Music of the Olive Tree

Every night during the summer months, Rabbi Adam Tibon of Yattir, born and bred in Upper Galilee, went walking through his grandparents olive grove for what the Kabbalists know as *tiqun ḥatsot* תיקון חצות, or midnight reparation. Sitting on a thick cushion he placed among the rocks, Rabbi Adam would look first at the stars, then at the aged trees, the skyline of Mount Meron and the ragged horizon. As a child, he had heard an Arab cobbler of Nazareth say that olive trees produced a strange and subtle music, a spiral music.

"I can understand that they twist upwards following the pattern of a rope," he would say aloud to himself, scratching his beard, "as if they showed in this way their bonding to sun and heaven, but as for the music..."

Intrigued, restless, he would time and again lean his ear against the rugged barks, and he would hug the trees, as if afraid to be missing the mysterious melody; but as he did not hear a thing, not even a quarter-tone that could be called music, he would feel frustrated, to the point that he would start doubting the truth of what Mafud, the cobbler, had told him. But after some years devoted to this practice, with pupils wide open on moonless nights, wrapped by darkness like a foetus by its placenta, he had the fortune to witness a meteor shower, which he naively interpreted as the opening of the gates of heaven, gates that had perhaps actually turned on their hinges by grace of his meditation. Such is solitude, that everything happening around us seems to be our responsibility.

Initially it was a murmur from the leaves, a spear-shaped rustling, a symmetrical swinging. Then rattlings turned into the sighing of boughs, and immediately the lonely chirp of a cricket, in whose metallic shrilling would quiver the joints of the world. After this experience, Rabbi Adam Tibon of Yattir was able to see without looking, feeling himself beyond the spinning wheel of riddles, and beyond the enigmas of the stone; beyond the forced blindness that the night imposed upon him; even beyond the botanical aspect of time, which had been growing those olives for centuries. He perceived the rhythm of his inner fire, the pattern in the sun's flames, which would sleep, and dream, and awaken later on in the burnt out firewood. And he could hear the fire rising up in spirals, flicking its rings, stretching out its tongues, savouring a rain-tasting sap, and quickening love particles in the air. Rabbi Adam saw all that, and then he heard how, clear and precise, the spiral music of the olive trees was encompassing the shadows with heartbeats of living wood, and how it was caressing the earth with roots of constancy.

"I understand now," he said to himself, as he stood up with a smile soaked in tears of joy, "I do understand now: I was unable to hear it while my silence was not deep enough for my fall into wonderment to match my absorption into the plenitude of the stars. You can see the fire whilst not hearing it, but you can also listen to the unlit flames. Imagination is a gradual treasure, revealed by reality without any method or system.

In the Hebrew name of the cricket, tsartsar צרצר, *are included the roots* tsar צר, *to give form, and* rats רץ, *to run. Perhaps, and simply, the secret music of the olive trees that Rabbi Adam thought he had heard, started by the insect, was the acoustic form of the stellar movement as reflected on those trees. Besides, by its gematric value, cricket or* tsartsar צרצר *(580) is equivalent to* saraf שרף *(580), no less than a seraph, the angel of fire!*

In Every Scroll of the Law

"In every scroll of the Law," Rabbi Na'um of Odessa once said to his disciples, "are stored hundreds of waves of the Spirit. Whenever we plunge into these waves, their foam of light breaks against our frontal lobes, refreshing our souls, and adding some salt to the blandness of our lives."

The students looked at him attentively, without blinking. The master had been made blind during a fire, when a blazing beam fell upon his head. He kept his blue eyes wide open, but his glance seemed to rest beyond, floating on the curve of the sea. He could see nothing, but he perceived everything; he could not tell colours or forms, but he would divine whether there was love, or sloth, or interest in the heart of his questioner.

"A wave is to the sea what man is to God. The manner in which deep water renews its oxygen upon contact with the air of its shores is as the way in which the Creator sees His designs fulfilled above the human horizon," the rabbi went on, as he moved slowly sidewards his oak walking cane. "The wave rises, aiming at a transparency not always reached, and it finally collapses, all energy lost, water upon water dissolved. Thus also, man rises, aspiring to move in ever clearer regions until, bending upon his years, he returns his image to the Creator, whose likeness he is."

The silence of the study house at that afternoon hour was pierced by a ship's distant siren coming from the harbour.

"That is a beautiful simile," said one of the students.

"Perhaps sad as well," said another.

"It is unquestionable," a third one stated.

"The Torah," smiled Na'um of Odessa at last, "is the best of planks for the worst of shipwrecks. So much so that it preserves between its scrolls all those waves which, from the outside, would be threatening our existence and sprinkling our fate with fear. The Torah, if you believe in its currents and if you sail down its passages, shall lead you away from deserted islands into the continents, and from these into their substance. Every single day, and for ever.

The Hebrew word megilah מגילה, *or scroll of the Law, hides between its syllables a* gal גל, *or the one wave capable of restoring us to the horizon of discernment; but since biblical readings are multiple and polysemic, we can speak, with true rigour, of waves or* galim. *Moreover, in the Hindu tradition the human being is a wave in the cosmic ocean, a brief and fleeting manifestation of its dancing totality. The Sanskrit term* rita *designates the cosmic order, disposition and providence, but also water and sacrifice.*

The Heart of Solitude

One of the daughters of Lo-Yadua, the Unknown, once reproached her father for enjoying his solitude so much, being as he was much more social than he wished to appear.

"It is as if," the young woman observed, "your happiness was never a collective fact, something you could share with others."

"That is not true," replied the master, "for everything is sharable, and everything is collective, even this solitude which seems to you overly lonely. Our prophet Isaiah has left for us the promise that the Creator shall change our human solitude for His garden, and this shows that unless we are near such a still way of living, near that special experience implied in our silence and the silence of others, we will not see the verdancy of Paradise, nor listen to the joyous singing of its birds."

"Why do you answer with someone else's sentence to a situation which is only yours?" his daughter insisted.

"Because the lonely heart of silence belongs to everyone, whereas the varying alternation of words and languages belongs to such and such a person. Isaiah spoke for you and for me, for whoever wanted to listen, be it in this century or the next."

"He may have meant to say," the girl insisted, "that we will be comforted in our solitude by the vision of ultimate beauty, Paradise, but not that one is to be exchanged for the other. Solitude is not, it seems to me, an exact equivalent of that garden which is so miraculous in the world of the imaginal."

"To interpret is to choose," the Unknown smiled. "Remember that the Scripture versets have no periods or commas, and that when we stop we don't do so because there is an indication, but because we can no longer continue. In the same way, if you fearlessly go across your solitude, if you enjoy it and receive its message, a path of heartbeats shall reveal its entrance into Heaven by making you share in the dance of its rotations. The day you understand the heart of solitude, the entire world seems to be cordial to you."

In Isaiah 51:3 we read: "For the Creator shall comfort Zion: He will comfort all her waste places; and He will make her wilderness like Paradise, and her solitude like the garden of Jehovah." But since the original text has no punctuation, we can indeed believe that the exchange here is of solitude for Paradise or, even more, that only through cultivating solitude can we perceive its delights. "The treasure presents itself as a quest," says Pseudo-Macarius, "until the entire universe is revealed as a finding."

Blood and Image

Rabbi Schmuel Handas of Bukhara used to take his students to the outskirts of Samarkand, to show them the ruins of an astronomical observatory which had been under the custody of his father for decades.

"My father learnt, by the sheer pleasure of praising, hundreds of names of stars," confided Rabbi Schmuel Handas to his disciples during one of those outings, "and he used to sing them to me on summer nights, when we sat at home on our veranda facing the dark, perfumed sky. It went thus:

> Sirrah, Mirach and Alamak,
> Algol, Deneb and Schedir;
> Pores of light on the dark body of God,
> Worlds sung by Him,
> Spheres by Him numbered.

"Then he would invariably place his heavy hand on my child's shoulder," the Rabbi continued, "and he would quote verse 9:6 of Genesis: 'Whoso sheddeth man's blood, by man shall his blood be shed: for in the image of God made He man.' And thus he disciplined my soul in peace and serenity, distancing me with his words from any quarrel and from every violent way."

"I do not see the connection between the stars and blood, Master," Amir of Fergana, his eldest disciple, then questioned him.

"Everything that burns and glimmers in the constellations is within your arteries and flows downstream in your veins, running through your interior," replied the master. "My father held that in each name, in every one of its sounds, the stars were proclaiming the glory of their Creator. Then he would take my heartbeat, thus making me aware of it, and he would teach me how to recite them, so that I would never forget the slow but persistent dripping of wisdom. 'In the night of your blood,' he said, 'white cells are stars, red cells are comets, and the iron atoms are planets. In the night of your blood He is always He Who Dawns by Himself'."

"Did he pronounce those names without knowing their meaning?" asked another of the disciples.

"Indeed," answered Rabbi Schmuel Handas, "neither do I know what they mean, but evoking them makes me so happy!"

Image and blood, tselem צלם *and dam* דם, *when combined, and once stripped of the final letter mem* ם *they have in common, form the word le-tsad* לצד, *meaning in favour of, at the side of. The wise man, Kabbalists say, takes before men the side of the Creator, and before the Creator the side of men.*

The Baker and the Angels

A baker from Cochin, a member of the Jewish community of the Bene Israel, dubbed by his friends "The baker of the angels", used to fashion every day, with the leftover dough, a replica of himself he would leave by night on the veranda of his house, for the night dew to moisten it, and for the morning dew to bring him blessings from afar. Apparently Simha Hineni, such was the name of the baker, used to introduce improvements as he kneaded his double, adding also ideas that would perfect his own inner life.

When finishing, as he delicately drew the navel, Simha Hineni would say:

"Take away the bad from me, and bring me the good from Him; undo my defects, and bring me all sorts of benefits."

But it seldom happened that Simha Hineni saw again his figure untouched on the veranda, for the ravenous birds called in India striated laughing thrushes, about the breaking of dawn, descended to feast upon the doughy little body of the angelic baker, with a cinnamon-coloured hustle and bustle.

"They have started with your eyes today," his neighbour Amos Nisim told him mockingly, as he spied from the house next door. "Tomorrow they may start with your secret parts, and as you rise from bed you may not have what to urinate with."

"Be silent," the baker invariably replied. "One day the angels will come, and feeding on my dough image they shall cheer my soul in its saddest quarters, replacing longings with joys, vanities with virtues."

On one occasion, wishing to make a joke, two boys sprinkled the baker's veranda with chicken's blood, and as he came to fetch the remains of his dough image from the night before, he felt injured, not knowing whence or from whom the damage came. Trembling with fear, he regarded the stains as a protest, and thus it was that the following night he laid himself down, back to the floor, on his veranda. He fell asleep until the hour in which the birds came for their daily ration; when they saw him, they were so surprised that they started squeaking and shrieking above their usual chirping.

"Here I am," he said to the striated laughing thrushes. "If you want anything else from me, you must ask me face to face."

A cheeky bird then alighted on his right shoulder, and confided the following:

"You have waited so long for the angels, that you have forgotten men. It is time that, instead of reproducing yourself, you distribute the surplus dough among those who can not even afford to buy flour. It is not from the image of oneself that improvements come, but from the one we form, with our thoughts and actions, in the eyes of others. Your neighbour grants you the measure of perfection you deserve, only in his service you have forgotten your own."

Simha Hineni never knew whose blood that was, nor who he had talked to, but he did not need to ponder much over what he had heard from the beak of the laughing thrush.

The striated laughing thrush (Turdoides striatus) *is well-known for its habit of staying in groups of six to eight individuals, and this is why it has at times received the name of* seven sisters, *and in certain zones of India* seven devas *or* angels, *who roam the earth in order to cleanse it of evil spirits. These birds, who are gregarious even during their breeding period, hold a constant communication amongst themselves, letting out whisper-like noises while they feed on insects or on human leftovers.*

The Sweetness of Wisdom

Gil ibn Hardon, a disciple of Menahem ben Saruq, chair of the Hebrew School of Cordova during the glory days of Muslim rule in 10th century Al-Andalus, wanted to know why his master always compared wisdom to honey whenever he had a chance to speak about this topic. Being a good student, he was familiar with the quotation from Proverbs 24:14, which over the centuries had given a base to such an association, but not having a sweet tooth, he struggled to understand how honey and wisdom could be synonyms.

"Like honey," Menahem ben Saruq explained at last under his insistence, "wisdom preserves us and preserves itself. It is fluid, golden, supple and practically endless. But the most interesting thing about it—I mean about honey—is that from a thousand flowers it becomes one single substance, from so many hues, petals and shades, one single colour. Wisdom also works this way: it will synthesise the essence of each problem, and offer you its solution when needed most. Beyond the complex swarm of daily affairs, and if you are ready to listen, the bees of words, once they have seized the honey of wisdom, shall fly always at your service."

Gil ibn Hardon and his master Menahem ben Saruq were sitting next to a pond where half a dozen green papyri were shooting out from the water. A solitary lotus was starting to reveal its summer blush above the surface.

"Besides," the master insisted, "if you are so lucky as our Samson to extract honey from a dead lion, if you are fortunate enough to transmute ferocity into subtlety, bestiality into nobility, then wisdom will not only be sweet to your mouth, but it will also be a remedy for other people's ills."

Mario Satz

Gil ibn Hardon's glance fell on one of the papyri. His eyes could not give credit to what they saw: light was splitting in two clearly different shafts at the papyrus, and travelling back towards the water fountain; now through the two shafts of light travelled three little humming bees. Thinking it was a trick from his master Menahem, a sheer illusion, Gil rubbed his eyes.

"What is obvious," ben Saruq remarked when he saw his gesture, "what is obvious is the honeycomb of the wonderful. Open it confidently, and eat from the sweetness of each revelation as if it had been sent to you from the bluest and farthest corner of heaven.

It is common in Hebrew culture to recall the relation between davar דבר *and* dvash דבש, *word and honey, two concepts distinguished only by the letters* shin ש *and* reish ר. *The combination of these two gives us the name for song or poetry,* shar שר. *There exists, furthermore, a semantic link between the bee,* deborah דבורה, *and* davar דבר, *word.*

Breathing In Infinity

As he lay the apricots of his little orchard out to dry under the blazing July sun, Rabbi Ovadia ben Adar of Izmir used to say:

"There is more sweetness in what shrinks and yet remains, than in the fruit which merely reacts to the water of the moment and the hunger of the hour. Such is also the age of a man who has been dehydrated by the sun, but who has been concentrated by love, giving him more flavour upon each new wrinkle, increasing him in mildness for every hint of a smile he can give before the abyss of death."

Golden as honey, the apricots were placed on the run-down edges of his veranda by the worn-out hand of the old rabbi. There they stayed until the sugar in them reached the ideal level, and that was the moment to sell them. Those blown to the ground by the wind were for the hens or for the beggars, but those which remained clean, tender and firm under the fierce sun became part of his meagre income.

Poverty was a privilege to him, widowerhood his strongest pain, and the relative distance from his children a relief. Ovadia had a goat, a mule and eighteen fruit trees with which he used to chat. The study house he attended was no richer or more comfortable than his own home, but it was white and spacious enough to accommodate in its inner courtyard some large pots of basil and chairs for his friends Rabbi Ishmael Duban and Rabbi Yosef Nissim.

"When between words and actions our breath perceives infinity," he confided once to his friends, "then wonder opens wide our mouth."

"I suppose that perceiving is taking notice," said Rabbi Ishmael.

"And that taking notice is feeling," added Rabbi Yosef Nissim. "But if you do not make yourself a little clearer, we shall not be able to solve the riddle you are posing."

Rabbi Ovadia then took the branch of his oldest apricot tree, which he had skilfully turned into a staff, and wrote on the ground two Hebrew words, meaning respectively *you* and *now*.

"Mark how the letters dance," he observed, pointing at what he had written over the floor covered in the finest sand. "See how their meanings go up and down. Breath is now where infinity was, and where infinity was, there is now the breath. Ask from your eyelids a blink, and understanding will come to you of its own. The moment that happens, in the instant your mind opens its transparent butterfly wings, your thoughts will be nowhere, and your head everywhere."

The words written by the master are the homophones ata' אתא *and atah* אתה, *the verb to come, to arrive presently, and the pronoun you. While the first one is closed by a final alef* א, *indicating infinity, the second word ends with a hei* ה, *token of breath and breathing; and yet both words share the beginning and the end of the alphabet. When the breathing recognises its heavenly provenance, our life-giving breath becomes truly admirable.*

The Lightning of Paradise

"I have come to think," Rabbi Isaac of Istanbul muttered softly to his grandson Yosef David, "I have come to think that we left Paradise after a storm, and that we shall return there in less than a flash of lightning."

They were drinking golden apple tea on the shores of the Bosphorus, and like every Saturday afternoon, they were walking together, chatting about this and that, as they watched the hustle of the fishing boats and they heard the distant, sinuous and magnetic voice of the muezzins singing their call to prayer.

"Why a storm, grandfather?" asked Yosef David.

"Everything must have darkened suddenly. The sky must have oppressed the earth," he carried on, half closing his eyes, "with criss-crossing thunders and broken winds. Then, when the horizon was so close that its line matched the profile of the lips of our ancestors, Eve and Adam realised that the rain had left wet and sad tears over the leaves, and that they had ahead of them a wide land to plough, a vast reality to assume, and their own hands to cope."

"I asked you why a storm," repeated his grandson, remembering that the old man was almost deaf.

"Because storms transmute secrets into revelations, and leaving Paradise was somehow a revelation which amounted to growing centuries old in seconds, millennia in a few instants. We had everything within us, but we did not realise anything; on the outside we had nothing, but we realised everything."

"You also said that we will return to Paradise in less than it takes a flash of lightning. Isn't it so?"

"And so it is," said the old rabbi, stroking his grandson's head. "So it is. In fact, the entire earth is a Paradise, but we have to go very far from it to be reminded of this by the nostalgia of its wonders. Until, on a given day—a different one for each of us—a stirring of lightning shall allow us to be everything without having anything and, once our steps are turning in the right direction, to be able to say, like you and me now: how beautiful the sea is, and how round the sun nesting in its waters."

"Is that Paradise? A fading glint of beauty?"

"You should better say an illusion flaring up," said the old rabbi, "beyond our eyes, there where the world has fallen so low that it starts rising anew.

The numerical value of Paradise, or Eden *(124), is indeed equivalent to that of* beziqah בזיקה *(124), a flash of lightning, and hence the correctness in the intuition of old Rabbi Isaac of Istanbul. In Chinese Buddhism there is also a relation between lightning and illumination, access to the non-dual or paradisal mind. They say that an erudite of the Sung dynasty (10th to 13th centuries), by the name of Zhaopian, was once sealing official documents in his studio when, upon hearing the powerful rumble of thunder, he felt that his mind opened like a flower, whiter than light, and then he wrote in celebration:*

> *Empty of thoughts, in silence I sat*
> *before my desk, facing a darksome sky,*
> *with unperturbed mind, serene as water.*
> *Suddenly the blast of thunder opened my senses completely,*
> *and there was the old man sitting in all simplicity.*

Likewise we read in the Kabbalistic classic Sefer Yetsirah *that, "Numbers (the figures in the world) correspond to the ten infinites; once they are perceived, they resemble lightning, and they are decidedly headed towards that which has no beginning and no end. It has been said of them that they rise and descend at the command of the Creator, that they dive as a hurricane and they bow down before His Throne" (chapter II, 1st paragraph). Also in the* Kena Upanishad *of the Hindus it is said, "This is the teaching regarding Brahman: flashing forth like lightning and disappearing in the wink of an eye" (4,4).*

The Power of the Listener

For forty years Abu Moses sold towels in the desert. In the company of his camel Little Mountain, he would roam oases and hamlets in order to inveigle to and convince nomads about the advantages of hygiene. They knew him as Al-Yehud, the Jew; and also as Al-Huruf, the Lettered One, on account of his obsession to always write on the sand the very same Hebrew word: *shema'*, listen, hear. Abu Moses had eyes scoured by storms and gales, and earlobes so long and hanging that he could have been taken for a Buddhist monk, had he not exhibited an unmistakably aquiline Jewish nose. His hands were as dark as his dusky face. Of middle height and powerful legs, Abu Moses loved in the darkness of coffee the beauty of the night, and in the transparency of tea the farewell of twilights. He knew a few prayers by heart, and these he never tired to repeat while having his meagre meals, raising his quick and high-pitched voice. At the end of those forty years on the roads, he had registered in his memory so many sounds, whispers and drip tones, that the dwellers of the desert had come to trust his forecasts and suggestions as to moving their herds or diverting their caravans. Whenever he appeared on top of a hill with his saffron umbrella, he was a cheerful sight for everyone, since Abu Moses, the one with storm-scoured eyes, carried with him, wrapped among his draperies, the caressing silence of peace.

Once in a while, his customers would ask him:

"Why do you always write the same word, Abu Moses?"

"So as not to fall too deeply into my own thoughts," replied the tradesman. "The wilderness I traverse is so full of songs of the breeze and moans of the wind, of eagle calls and the punctuation of insects, that I have come to hear, in the quiet of dawn, and in the loving scrape of lizards, the green promises of oncoming spring. Once I got to hear the birth of gold within the rock veins, and on another occasion I heard the pace of the rain over the dunes. One morning—and this was long ago—I heard the crystalline crackling of the sand under the hooves of a hundred horses, and that same day the potency of the One was in the booming of thunder. I can, if I set about doing so—but words would not suffice—I can differentiate more than ten tones within one single sound, and even ten distinct sounds within one chirp. This is because what you call hearing—I mean really hearing, you must believe me—is a rare art in which initially you expect to find an echo of your name in everything, only to realise in the end that no one ever says his name in the desert."

"How is this?" his listeners would enquire.

"It is very simple: the desert sky is so transparent, and its emptiness so void, that under its vault your 'I' vanishes at every breath. You become so eager for something to break the apparent monotony of your advance, that the slightest colour variation in the landscape, or the softest rustle of acacia leaves, intimate a hundred answers before you have even asked your first question."

"And these answers, what do they say?"

"Oh, as often as not they will say the same thing: 'Hear, O Israel: our God is One.'"

"Is that all?"

"No, of course not. They also say, 'Let your eye follow your ear, lest your pupil leads your hearing astray, and you end up where you ought not to be, finding what is not for you.'"

The invocation in Deuteronomy 6:4: 'Hear, O Israel: the Eternal, our God, is One,' has so many levels of interpretation as diverse as the sounds making up its words. To start with, shema' שמע, *hear, can be read as* shem שם, *name, and* 'ain ע, *the eye, hence the advice for the sight to follow the ear, and not the opposite. Besides, given its numeric value,* shema' שמע *(410) equates with* qadosh קדוש, *the holy, the sacred. Everything is at once One and holy, sacred, worthy of admiration and respect. Now, if we transpose the sounds of* shema' שמע, *we can obtain the word* 'emas עמס, *to carry, to burden, and hence that in order for our burden to be lighter, we must "listen" to what it contains, looking at it as if from the inside out. As regards the Divine One, eḥad* אחד, *some masters interpret it, on the human level, as He who is* aḥ את, *brother, relative, and* ḥad חד, *subtle, fine, sharp, and piercing to everything existing. Then, if considered well, then, species and spices are subtly fraternal under the blue sky of the Father.*

To See the Light, to Be the Light

"It is one thing to see the light," said Rabbi Gedalia of Kabul, the wool-buyer, "and a different one altogether to be the light."

The children listening to him had large, black olive eyes. If it was difficult to teach them how to sing the Psalms, it was even harder to have them pay attention to their contents. Especially during the summer, when bunches of golden grapes were laid out on the market stalls in the sun, and when the bronze ding-dong of the tamarind juice seller would open their thirsty mouths.

"In Psalm 36:10 we read: 'In Thy light shall we see light.' Will someone here explain to me what is the deeper meaning of this sentence?" Master Gedalia went on.

Laughter came to a halt, elbows were called to awaken, eyelids came to a standstill.

Beyond the study hall—which smelled of wool and pistachio, of nuts and pitch—voices and calls were heard. Their location, a poor quarter of Kabul, was an island of meaning, the refuge of ancestral dreams, the space to invoke spirits, and to play with the straightness or sinuosity of the letters.

"First we must see the Creator outside ourselves," started a shy-looking boy called Zecher by the others on account of his enviable memory, a child who would eventually become the famous Rabbi Uriel of Kabul, "then to understand that we are seeing him through our eyes, and finally to ascertain that these go from the inside out."

"Would this imply that light dwells as much in the inside as on the outside of our heads?"

"It is thus, Master," replied a tall and curly-haired teenager.

THE LIVING PALM TREE

"And then, my dear ones, coming back to my first reflection, what will it mean to be the light?"

"To have so much happiness under the skin, so much sun in our hands, so much joy in our hearts," said the future Rabbi Uriel of Kabul without knowing what he was saying, overcome by a sudden enthusiasm, "so many sparkles in our laughter, so many gleams on our forehead, and so much surprise in our soul, that if we were in a dark room we would be a lamp for the others, their human lamp, the flame to soothe their shadows."

Some praised his memory, others patted his back. The master, astonished, asked him:

"Who has taught you all this, Uriel?"

"Words are a river, and they carry me," answered the one called Zecher. "And when this word river meets the sea of the Torah, I open my mouth, as if it is no longer mine, to let time speak—I mean, the generations that have preceded us. My life is other lives, as my lips are other lips."

"This is being the light," the master remarked. "This is what it is to be like light beyond what light itself differentiates."

The psalm in question affirms: "In Thy light shall we see light," be-orcha nireh or באורך נראה-אור, *suggesting that between divine light and human act are deployed, separated by a tiny space, the two letters of the word* ken כן, *yes, and also, with the same spelling,* kan כן, *here, right here, whence that only through a positive, open and synchronic attitude are we allowed to see the immense and cosmic within the small and human. To see the light is an obvious fact; to be the light, a hidden certitude.*

Punishment and the Hands

One afternoon in Jerusalem, Lo-Yadua, the Unknown Rabbi, heard from his master, whom everyone called the Ancient of Days on account of his incomparable white hair, that the left hand embodies punishment, while the right one embodies mercy. Through the large window-pane of the study house you could see the soft uneven snow falling. The old master had had an argument with his wife, and his face showed affliction. The big age gap between the pair would not yield to the harassments of time or to the timing differences in their biorhythms.

"If it is so," answered Ariel the Talmudist, one of his students, "you should tell her to have mercy with her right hand, given that she has judged you harshly with her left."

"Ah," the Ancient sighed, "you do not know, perchance, what Shams, the master of Rumi the Persian, said regarding the wives of the philosophers?"

The books were closed, the afternoon darkened, the tea kettle came to a boil.

"If one of the members of the couple is more studious than the other," the Ancient of Days went on, "and therefore slower to anger, and more cautious as to judgment, there is no way the other will not always win and impose his or herself in every discussion. If she is right, there is nothing to be done; if she is not, there is nothing I can do anyway, because her temper has taken her somewhere else, and thus, how will she be paying for a debt she will not remember she ever contracted!"

The disciples comforted him as best they could, and on the following day, the Unknown decided to intervene on behalf of the Ancient. He went over to their house, he waited for the master

THE LIVING PALM TREE

to go to walk the dog, and he surprised the woman in the kitchen. Considering that his visits were frequent, she was not alarmed. She asked him to come in and she said her husband would be back shortly. The Unknown One sat by the bookshelf and started reciting:

> If you hit with one hand,
> Prepare the other for a prompt caress,
> Since the longer the distance
> Between punishment and pardon,
> The less effective the corrective will be,
> And the less sweet will pardon's taste be
> For those who are to savour it.

That very night, before sleep, the wife of the Ancient remembered the words of the most beloved disciple of the master, and she caressed the old man's head while he slept, with a renewed patience. She thought that as hard as it could be, their living together was, and would continue to be, the greatest of miracles.

The Blessing of the Food

Rabbi Levi of Alexandria asked Rabbi Razi of Elephantine why it is that foods need to be blessed, to which Razi replied:

"Gratitude tempers sacrifice, just as the awareness of what you are eating gives depth to the flavour of what goes through your mouth."

During those years, in the 2nd century of our era, under the Greek rule of Egypt, food was scarce, but it was agreeable, as much as, or even more than, the time spent by the river watching the ducks play or the dragonflies darting in pairs. The two friends had chosen the shade of a sycamore to sit down and talk. Some boats, with their red or violet sails, were transporting sailors' songs, animals and bales of grass.

"My master, Rabbi Eliahu of Joppe," observed Razi, "said that every food requires a particularly suitable blessing."

"For example?" asked Levi of Alexandria.

"For grapes, it is not enough to say 'the fruit of the vine,'" observed Razi. "We should also tell them: 'We give thanks for every drop of rain you did not let fall, that you trapped under the green transparency of your skin, sweetening it for the delight of our mouths and for the joy of the birds.'"

"I see what you mean," Levi said. "According to this, when we get a pomegranate, we should say: 'With thanks for the reflection of twilight on your grains, for the rosy light you keep, for not letting it die, and thanks for the firmness with which you keep your gleams together.'"

"So it is," Razi continued. "*The soul is the manna of the body*, a Biblical delicacy which, as you know, comes from the Highest. Thus, when we bless foods from within her, the mother of our tongue, we are raising them and revealing how miraculous they are, since the greatest work of man is to join what is scattered, and to give a voice to that which is silent."

"Bless this date," asked Levi from Razi with a smile, as he offered him one, thus prompting him to look for inspiration in the palm tree, the desert and the sun.

"Thank you for teaching us," the man from Elephantina sighed, "that wrinkles are something more than dry rigours, and that the darkness sinks between your creases only in order to further concentrate your flavour. Thank you, date, for showing us your innocent perfection."

When they finished talking, the first star bore witness to its own radiation on the water, and it took back to heaven a more fluent look.

The Reader of Clouds

There lived in Damascus, around the third decade of the last century, a humble Jewish cobbler who, as chance and the contempt of the police would have it, was jailed for a crime he did not commit, a crime which was all the more horrendous in the eyes of the judges, given the Jewish piety of the accused, whose religious zeal was well-known by all his neighbours. Haim Anan—this was his name—knew by heart the Psalms and the Song of Solomon, and he used to recite them in the synagogue and during the feasts, for his voice was a wonder of grace, with the quality of an oboe and the texture of silk. To be a Jew in modern Syria was never easy, but it became a Calvary soon after the State of Israel came to existence. Twenty generations of Anan had lived in Damascus before the innocent Haim, and it is certain that if he had had a chance to leave the city for a better fate, he would have quickly declined it in order to keep smelling the cardamom fragrance of his shop's alley, the acrid glue smell, and the harsh aroma of the leather pieces no one would now use. He was arrested between one and two in the morning, as he devoted himself to *tiqun ḥatzot* תיקון חצות, or the midnight reparation, as recommended by the masters of Safed.

They stopped him without questions or any explanations, and they threw him into a dark cell from which—he had forgotten when—they moved him to a forced labour camp outside the city. As he had no relatives other than some distant cousins, and these afraid they might fall victim to new injustices if they interceded on his behalf, the small Jewish community of his neighbourhood forgot him soon enough.

Haim Anan requested a prayer book in Hebrew, his *tallit* or heavenly prayer shawl, and a pencil and paper to write, and all these were refused. Every time he insisted on his innocence and asked for a copy of the Bible, or at least an Arabic translation of the Book of Genesis or the Book of Proverbs, he received the following sarcasm in answer:

"Read the clouds, read the air. You must consider the bars of your cell window as the vertical lines of a narrow page. You will never leave this place, Jew."

At dawn, in summer as in winter, he was taken out along with the other inmates to the quarry where they extracted stones for the rich people's houses. Haim's eardrums had been damaged by the explosions, by the hammering, and by the iron picks scratching the mountain sides. The day he forgot himself, when he stopped thinking where he was and why, that very day the clouds started taking shapes before his eyes, against the blue background that gave them origin and where they would eventually return, shapes of letters, resemblances of Biblical passages, appearances of versets, faces of legendary characters such as Jacob or Samson, Deborah or Batsheva. It was enough for him to raise his eyes to the sky during the breaks, or between two hammer blows, to read the flight of the clouds and decipher joys marching towards the promise of rains or a simple travelling sunshade.

This was a secret he shared with no one, an unexpected event which he received as a relief from above for his sufferings here below. In spring, at the time of sunset, while the swifts circled fifty, perhaps eighty times around the same place beyond the little window of his cell, the clouds told him: "This is a cold downward current," "The ants are a wise people," or "Love God with all your soul and all your heart." Haim would read them effortlessly, one by one, not knowing whether he looked at cirri, cirrostrati, altocumuli or altostrati. One morning he saw an anvil-shaped cumulus, and behind it the image of Judas Maccabeus, the Hammer; another morning he saw the rising of a tempest, speaking to him about the Red Sea and Moses. Even in his dreams he would read clouds, very thin clouds vanishing into shreds, exceedingly white, like the breasts of doves. Haim Anan was ignorant of there being four basic kinds of clouds whose various combinations give warning of the weather conditions divined by meteorologists, but even so, he knew their evolution towards rain, or the light creases in their edges signalling higher winds.

He came to believe he himself was a dark cloud, one under which still stood, impeccably clean, the abode of the Creator. On the feather-like cirri he would read geese migrations; on the clouds formed by ice needles that he could only surmise, he would see the ageless beards of the prophets, stroked on their way towards bliss. He gradually forgot about the existence of books, with their accumulation of obedient signs, their periods and their marks. No letter stayed in his memory longer than the fleeting transit of an altocumulus in its sinuous advance. In winter, with the fog, a tone of sombre sadness crept through his window looking for his rigid coach, but in its airy shape he read a change of season, the winter solstice in the days of Abraham, and with Isaac he set about to study the terrain for the deployment of troughs or drinking containers, barely noticing that the light bulb in his room grew fainter and fainter every day. And so, as his prison years went by like the clouds, his reading of them became so precise that wardens would ask him about the weather, and they would then place bets on his predictions, where there was hardly any trace of error.

"Hey, Jew," they would tell him, "read for me the clouds and the weather for Wednesday."

And after a brief minute's silence spent looking through the bars, Haim Anan's answer would emerge:

"The fronts will open, and the dawn sky will be born perfect, but at midday the clouds will join in a grey sea whose waves will not move until the night has come."

Thus he earned their respect—but not their admiration, nor their affection. They were wary of his visionary ability, of his destiny as human thermometer, of his mercurial character, and of his eyes enraptured in the reading of the clouds. Finally, two decades from his first day of prison, a full pardon came, as inexplicable as the exchange of prisoners whereby, three days later, he woke up in a kibbutz near Rosh Hanikra, by the Lebanese border.

"Welcome home, Haim," a man, tall and rustic, told him. "Our children need someone to repair their shoes." He spoke to him in Hebrew, then in Arabic, and finally in French.

By this time, his beard and sparse hair had a fantastic glow, even more noticeable against his dark features. His teeth were all intact, and he wept the first time they took him to gaze at the sea. He cried with joy, for above the horizon, spreading in fine, white stripes he could read the passage from Kings 8:12, where it is said that the Creator "loves to dwell in the mist" and makes of clouds His permanent abode, since nothing could enclose or contain Him, as is recorded on the occasion of the inauguration of the Temple of Solomon. They had not been able to turn him, Haim Anan the cobbler, into a mere number, neither had they been able to take from him his age-old reading habits, his devotion to his own past.

"Do you like the sea, Haim?" the children asked every time they went to the beach with him and saw him shedding tears.

"Yes," he replied aloud, while in a whisper he added: "The Creator draws with clouds astounding and fleeting wonders of beauty, and the wind scatters and the weather allocates these subtle marvels. Half of my life I have been a cobbler, and another half a cloud reader. Thus, having aided the foot to bend its walk upon the earth has allowed my head to meditate on the sky. Blessed be He, Draughtsman of the winds, blowing breezes into the attentive ears of the grass."

Putting Heart In

"Of all the ways of paying attention," Rabbi Abraham of Tripoli said to his disciples, "of all our conscious attitudes, not one compares to putting heart into what we think, feel and do."

There were three of them walking together: Rabbi Yosef ben Mulk of Benghazi, Rabbi Adam of Sabha, and the master of them both, Rabbi Abraham. They walked by the edge of the desert under the mauve light of a Saturday afternoon. All three carried with them basil sprigs to perfume their steps; all three were grandfathers, and they had known each other for a long time.

"In that case, such attention will be fleeting, like a heartbeat," remarked Rabbi Adam of Sabha.

"Everything is fleeting," smiled Rabbi Abraham.

"However it may be," intervened Rabbi Yosef ben Mulk of Benghazi, "heartbeats do not leave the heart: they stay in it, similar to alternating birds, one of light, the other of shadow."

"All things possess shadow and light," smiled again Rabbi Abraham of Tripoli, "but not everything has a heart, for having a true heart requires celebrating, above all, movement, then stillness; ascension, then repose."

"You are making it really hard for us," observed Rabbi Adam of Sabha.

The afternoon colour changed from mauve to blue. One after another, the stars twinkled over the nearby desert.

"You present your enigmas as someone who hides his wings after having flown," said Yosef ben Mulk.

"Look," Rabbi Abraham said finally, taking out a plum from one of his pockets, a plum so much like a dove's heart that the three friends shivered at the acuteness of the resemblance. "Even a fruit heart like this is sweet in its surface and sour in its centre. In the same way, when asked to pay attention, we must use kindness to our fellows, and reserve sourness for ourselves, for sweetness lowers our eyelids in the same measure as what is sour opens our pupils. The attention deserved by others is called consolation; the exercise of our own attention is called awakening devotion."

The Hebrew expression sim leb שים לב, *to pay attention, can also be understood as putting heart into what we are doing. Besides, if we read* bal בל, *not, a negation, instead of* leb לב, *whose affirmation is implicit, we would be giving precedence to the static* bet *before the dynamic lamed. At the same time, the letter lamed* ל *signals an ascent, a climb, while* bet ב *furthers stability; hence that in the way of the realisation of the heart we must first learn how to get under way, and finally learn how to be at ease.*

The Living Palm Tree

As he was pushed into the abyss on a cold morning of May, 1944, Rabbi Ismach Atid was in his mind giving the final touches to the story he would have liked to write: about the end of General Vespasian, responsible for the destruction of Jerusalem, who was undone by madness somewhere out in the far reaches of the Roman Empire. "How foolish of me," he thought, "that walking towards death is making me remember that murderer, when no extinction will pay the price of extinction, when no punishment, however deserved, will restore a life." In the camp, surrounded by sallow faces and tear-emptied eyes, everyone seemed to be beyond thought, striped ghosts of themselves. Most of these souls were dead even before their bodies were exposed to the lethal gas—as dead as were already their beloved ones.

Rabbi Ismach Atid looked up to the sky searching for a signal, some sign of that craze which was destroying the entire human race, not only the Jewish people. But above the horror destined for some, Spring insisted on carrying aromas to others, as if the Creator of the universe, that being he still called God and whom he loved beyond any explanation, took pleasure in perfuming the air with floral essences above the stench of charred meat. "What a trifle," Rabbi Ismach Atid said to himself, "to think of writing something about Vespasian and the destruction of the Temple after all the history gone by, when the present is casting such a shadow of desolation over the future."

And then, woven in the thinnest of clouds, he saw a transparent, living palm rising to heaven from the deadly chimneys. And within it the warm souls of the righteous, the ethereal heart of the innocent ones, ascending in funereal eddies, drawing branches and spadices; and he saw a trunk so tall and slender, that it seemed made of the cotton from the dreams of the carbonised children... until two burning tears, flowing out ghastly and silent, blurred his perception. It was beautiful like life, and terrible like unwanted death, this palm tree, foretelling a sort of posthumous miracle on the horizon of a continent ravaged by the hordes of war. Following a vertical order, a mysterious aspiration in the rings of its trunk, travelled names and indelible memories, words of love and promises; and the souls lingered and lingered among the arms of this pale smoke, giving one another a glow as intense as unforgettable. Was he perhaps, Rabbi Ismach Atid, the only one to see them?

Before entering the gas chamber, he uttered a wish under his breath: "May this faint and hesitant transparent palm have a destiny worthy of remembrance, and may the righteous ones who compose it tell the angels that they long to return in the rays of the sun. All the darkness of the universe, O Lord, shall not conquer the light of Your stars."

Index

accusative, 126
Adam Kadmon, 91
adamah, 56, 137
adamah, 77
ain, 77
air (*avir*), 93, 121
alef, 8, 56, 77, 139, 155
aleph, 127
Allah, xvi, 29, 43, 44
alone (*lebad*), 63
animals; talking to, 28
arets, 56

Baal Shem Tob, 92, 121, 122
barakah, 43
baraqah, 75
Basho, Matsuo, 74
beekeeper, 43
Ben Yehudah, Eliezer, 125
bet, 172
birds, 65, 73, 151
blessing, 44, 165
blindness, 95
Book of Splendour, *see zohar*
breath, 122, 123, 130, 154, 155
Buddhism, xxii, 22, 157
building, 109

Cairo Genizah, 138
calligrapher, 29, 45
carob, 97
centre, 132
chance, 41
China, xvii, 157
cloud, 168
colour (*tseba'*), 35

community (*kehilah*), 100
Cossacks, 33
cricket (*tsartsar*), 143
crystals, 15
cube (*qubiyah*), 42
cure, 49
cyclic history, 29

dabar, 86
dan, 50
ad-Darqawi, 'Abd al-Qadir, xvi
death, 28, 54, 106, 113
deeds, 117, 134
delight, 50, *see 'ednah*
desert (*midbar*), xvii, 28, 58, 86, 131, 133, 138, 158
dew (*tal*), 32, 69
dialogue (*saḥ*), 37
diamond, 67
dim'ah, 77
dimayon ha-nefesh, 27
dragon (*teli*), 89

Eben Tabon, 126
echo, 48
Eden, 50
'ednah, 50
El Elohim, 42
Eloah, 63
emet, 46
Essenes, xviii, 129
et, 126
eternity, 116
Ezekiel, 27

family, 129

farming, 18
fear (*yir'at*), 19
feather, 29, 30, 45
Felashas, 134
firefly, 43
flash (*beziqah*), 157
flower, 107
food, 165
fool, 112
fortress (*tsur*), 6

gahal, 44
gahlilit, 44
gil, 44
gilgul neshamot, xxi
glory (*hod*), 48
grace, see *hen*
grace (*hen*), 21

haburah, 7
haftarah, 66
hamesh, 4
hands, 163
happiness, 3, 9
hashmal, 9, 11
Hasidism, xxii, 4, 92, 121
hayot, 27
hearers of silence, 95
heart, 46, 63, 103, 116, 172
hei, 2, 8, 48, 122, 155
hen, 22
Heraclitus, 60
Hinduism, 106, 145, 151, 157
hochmah nisteret, 22
Holocaust, 173
honey (*dvash*), 153
hourglass, 51
hozer, 59

Ibn Khaldun, 29
idiot, 54, 78, 112
immanence, 70
innovation, 29
Isis, 65

Japan, 74

Jesus, xvii
joy, 44, see *gil*

kiss, see *neshiqah*
Kotsuji, Setsuzo, 74

lamed, 172
language, 101, 127
lashon, 4, 46
leb, 105
light, 139
light (*or*), 80, 93, 139, 162
lightning, see *baraqah*
lime tree (*tirzah*), 120
love (*ahabah*), 32

Maat, 46
manah, 2, 49, 165
manna, 49, see *manah*
Mantiq ut-Tayr, 41
marriage, 163
Masada, 129
master, 141
mediation, 52, 84, 149
mem, 86
memaleh maqom, 70
memory, 139
mercy, 163
midnight reparation, 142, 167
Midrash, xxii, 45
minei, 2
mirror, 20
Mishnah, 54, 110
moon, 109
Moses, 23, 45, 58, 66, 109
Moses de Leon, xxi
moss (*tahab*), 84
mother-of-pearl (*dar*), 118
music, 143
Muslim, 43

Nag Hammadi, 138
name (*shem*), 60
neshiqah, 23, 36, 75
night (*lailah*), 28
nimah, 2

Noah, 14, 48, 81
nose, 8
nose (*af*), 8
notzah, see feather
numerology, 17

olive, 142
onion, 103
Operation Moses, 133
Or Torah, 126
Osiris, 65
ostrich, 45
oznei sheqeṭ, 95

Paradise, 7, 8, 50, 110, 133, 134, 146, 147, 156
patience, 164
pleasure, see *'ednah*
profane, 52
Psalms, xv, 5, 27, 28, 47, 73, 117, 122, 161, 167
psychostasis, 46

qarqa', 56
qen, 23
quill, 29, 45
Qumran, 128
Qur'an, 30

reading method, 18
reish, 139
remez, 88
repose, 21
repose (*noaḥ*), 22
ruaḥ, 97

Sabbath, 26
sacrifice, 45
Safael, 125
sagi nahor, 95
sand, 52
scroll (*megilah*), 145
seagull, 37
seeing, 16
Sefer Yetsirah, 40, 74, 89, 157
Sefer Ha-Bahir, xviii, 89, 118

seven sisters, 151
Shabbat, 105
shalom, 60
Shekhinah, 100, 101
Shema, 104, 113, 158, 159
shibah, 23
shibolet, 105
shomem, 4
simḥah, 4, 11
sleep, 120
slowness, 79
smile, 50, 113
soap, 14
sofer stam, 45
solitude, 147
stars, 148
Stone of Discernment, 126
stork, 27
storm, 157
stroll (*ṭiyul*), 69
Sufism, xv, 20, 29
surrender, 99
swallow (*dror*), 65

tallit, 129, 167
Talmud, xxi, xxii, 3, 7, 22, 37, 45, 62, 66, 70, 112
Tanakh, 31, 119
tariqah, xvi
tau, 20, 91, 127
tears, 76
Tetragrammaton, 32, 48, 91
Tetramorph, 11
thirty-two paths, 105
thunder, 157
tiqun ḥatzot, 142, 167
tithe, 45
tongue, see *lashon*
Torah, xix, xxii, 5, 18, 25, 30, 31, 33, 35, 45, 68, 70, 73, 74, 83, 94, 100, 102, 113, 119, 125, 129, 144, 162
travel, 132
Tree of Good and Evil, 7
Tree of Life, 7, 33, 34
truth, see *emet*
tsadiq, xv, 52

tsimtsum, 89

vav, 139
vav, 14, 89
Vespasian, xix, 173

weighing of the soul, 46
word play (*mitshaq milim*), 35

ya'en, 46
yesh, 24
yesod 'olam, 52
yod, 2
yod, 89, 93

Zodiac, 89
zohar, 59
zohar, xxi, 2, 7, 18, 98, 110, 111, 120

www.ingramcontent.com/pod-product-compliance
Lightning Source LLC
LaVergne TN
LVHW012058090426
835512LV00033B/138